MW01658508

Broken To Be Made Whole

Revised
By

CHERYL BASS-FOSTER

Foreword by Dr. Mary Ann Echols, Ph.D.

Copyright © 1992, 1993, 1994, 1996, 2000, 2015, 2020
by Cheryl Bass-Foster

ISBN: 978-0-936369-64-7

All rights reserved. This story or any portion thereof may not be reproduced or used in any manner whatsoever without the express written permission of the publisher except for the use of brief quotations in a book review.

Unless otherwise noted, all scripture quotations are taken from the Holy Bible, the King James Version.

Lessons from healing conferences will be cited.

All quotations from other authors are indicated throughout the text and credited.

All sermon excerpts are quoted or paraphrased as well as prophecies. Excerpts of counseling sessions are included by permission from the therapists for educational purposes.

Cover Design By Sherry Wyne

TABLE OF CONTENTS

DEDICATION

This book is dedicated to The Lord, our God and Savior, Jesus Christ.

"He healeth the broken in heart, and bindeth up their wounds." Psalms 147:3

To everyone who desires to be healed and made whole by the supernatural

Hand of God.

SPECIAL THANK YOU

Luther Foster Jr., my husband, for your unconditional love for over twenty-nine years. God used you to help make dreams come true. You are a phenomenal husband, dad, grandpa and great grandpa who have taught us unconditional love. I love you.

I love you, Juanita Shawnie Thompson, my daughter. You gave me a purpose for living through many broken years, and your love and support of fifty-one years, still amazes me. You gave me a wonderful birthday trip and surprise 70th birthday celebration that I'll never forget. I want to give you a special 50th Birthday shout-out.

I love you, Maya C. Bass, my granddaughter. You have a big heart, just a sweetheart of a person, loving, kind and very creative like your mother, just expressed in different ways.

I thank God for you Mom, for your love and for sharing your wisdom of 95 years and still counting. Thank you for giving Dad the family that he never had for 61 ½ years until his death. I love you.

In memory of my Daddy, O'Dell Nelson, who was one of a kind. He was a good and tough father who taught me, Butch, Denise, Darrell and Rex, many lessons on work ethics and how to fight to survive in this world. We still miss you every day.

Dr. Spencer and Marcetta Rhoades-Gaines, my "Lifetime" brother and sister-in-love. You provided unconditional love and hospitality, during our Rest & Recuperation in your beautiful home. Jacksonville, Florida is our favorite Happy Place that healed us through our grieving process that preceded our trip, and prepared us for multiple, unexpected losses of beloved friends following our visit. I love you.

Louis Sr. and Cleo along with Louis Rollins Jr., my brother, sister and nephew-in-love, you brought back so many family memories and laughs regarding your brother, Benny, until all of us healed. There's no pain left in the memories. I truly enjoyed the family reunion you initiated for me with Mike, James, Carrie, Mary, Ronnie and the rest of the family. We will return and continue where we left off, when we return to Jacksonville. I love you.

Bishop Willie Thornton, my spiritual son, you are wise beyond your years. I am in awe how God has used you in ministry since you was eight years old and in spite of your worldwide ministry to the nations, you always find time to attend every special occasion we have and keep in touch for decades. I respect and love you.

Elder Joseph S. Bowers, my spiritual son, you continued to dream dreams, and you kept hope alive, by continually sharing the vision, regarding God's intention for the books He inspired me to write. Thank you for those delicious pots of homemade soup hand delivered every flu season. I love you, Hope and Ariona.

Evangelist Katrina Mitchell, there are no words that can express your ministry of love and hospitality that you rendered to us in your home. We were able to be replenished during our many rest and recuperations. I love and thank you.

Pastor C. Shawn Tyson and First Lady Krista M. Tyson, you are anointed preachers and teachers who have guided Calvary through many broken places and for that I'm eternally grateful with great love and respect. I love you.

Bishop Chorrethers M. Jenkins, you have adopted us as your second family and have always been kind and supportive. I will never forget the move of God at Grace Evangelistic Temple on that weekend of Warrior Woman Breakthrough to The New You 2018. I love you.

Dr. Mary Ann Echols you are indeed an anointed Mental Health Wellness Therapist for the 21st Century move of God. Your wisdom is endless and your dedication to God-centered wellness shifted me into my God-given purpose, healing and wholeness. I will always be grateful and love you.

Pastor Martha Taylor and Vanessa Darby, for the monthly Women's Community ministry at Metro-Assembly during my restoration season for the past three years. The enthusiasm, inclusiveness and support will never be forgotten. Thank you and the sisters for your love and kindness. I love you.

Sister Sherry Wyne, all I can say is your incredible gift of kindness and creativity is beyond words and just keeps on giving. I marvel at how God does what He does through you and may He bless every one of your anointed books. Thank you once again for both cover designs.

To the incredible staff at the Davis branch of the Y.M.C.A. Thank you for providing such a warm, nurturing environment fostering holistic healing. To the incredible women who assisted me at this Inner Healing Day Spa, what a best kept secret in the Mahoning Valley. Powerful!

To Guy Sebastian, my former student, you have made the rewards of teaching worth every moment. Bishop Norman L. Wagner would be very proud of you now watching you facilitate Celebrate Recovery. I love you, Guy.

The Warrior Woman Committee Members, Team Members, The Crew, Warrior Men, Community Guests (Community Corrections, Beatitude House, Norman Carter House, The Rescue Mission), Sponsors, Donors, and Registrants we will never forget the powerful move of God., with great love. I love you.

In Memory of Warrior Women Bernadette Treece, Kathy Williams, Betty Williams, Carol Christian Brown and Yvette Woods. You have fought a good fight, you have finished your course, and kept the faith and have transitioned from labor to rest. Rest In Peace. RIP. We love and miss you.

We are praying for Warrior Woman Pamela Sumpter in the sudden loss of her son ,Mark, for her family's strength and healing during the grieving process.

There are so many others whose names are included in this book or the previous books. I love you.

FOREWORD

The request to write this Foreword to **Broken to be Made Whole: Breakthrough to the New You** by Cheryl Bass Foster came as both a pleasant surprise and a tremendous honor. I am honored by the opportunity to support the ministry of Cheryl Bass-Foster. Beyond that, I am humbled and honored to have been a part of the emotional healing and spiritual growth of this powerful woman of God.

Having known Cheryl Bass-Foster for many years as counselor and friend, and having read the first edition of **Broken to be Made Whole**, my understanding of and appreciation for the wisdom in this book has deepened. I can say, unequivocally, that this book represents the deep, no-holds-barred, painful but inspired, accounts of a life broken, healed and restored to wholeness by the matchless power of the Almighty God.

It leaves no doubt about how she made it through. Nothing was sugar coated. This extensive and in-depth account of her lifelong struggles explains in graphic detail how she was misused, abused, wounded deeply and how she descended into a downward spiral of misery and brokenness.

Bass-Foster kicks the lid off of pretense and pride and details the challenges and pitfalls of trying to cope with the stark realities of family dysfunction, addiction of loved ones, rejection, abuse, self-doubt, self-loathing and lost identity. She gives accounts of some of her most damaging experiences in life, love and suffering while also showing a deepening relationship with God and a greater awareness of her true identity.

She shows step by step how her false victim identity steeped in hurt and anger was cast off and she was able to embrace her true identity as a child of God wrapped in love, power and peace. But, praise God. The story doesn't end there. Perhaps this book was written, revised and updated to reach new generations of individuals who are hiding in the darkness of silent pain. If that is you, you need to know that there is a way out. But, the way out must begin with awareness and understanding of the truth about pain and suffering. Part of that truth is that (for the child of God) there is always purpose in the pain (God's purpose).

Broken to be Made Whole illustrates that, regardless of whether the source of your pain is uncontrollable circumstances, rejection, abandonment, abuse by others, or whether you brought on your own misery by poor decisions, poor choices or self-will, God desires to rescue you, receive you as His own and heal you. He is able to make something beautiful out of the suffering, fulfill his purpose and plan for your life, and restore you to wholeness.

Broken to be Made Whole epitomizes the lessons of Psalms 51 when King David acknowledges his sin and pleas for restoration with God. In that passage David said "Behold I was shapen in iniquity and in sin did my mother conceive me. Behold, thou desirest truth in the inward parts: and in the hidden part thou shalt make me to know wisdom (Verses 6-7).' The sad but subtle truth about brokenness and healing is that you have to go deep and honestly confront the truth before healing can take place. You must surrender the hurt and anger, humble yourself, and accept the reality of your brokenness before you can be made whole.

The beauty and power of being broken to be made whole is in the process itself which gives wisdom through the powerful work of the Holy Spirit. Anyone who has experienced abuse, rejection, hurt or violence can benefit from reading this book. Anyone who has been caught up in a web of family dysfunction, addictions or abusive relationships and want emotional and spiritual freedom will find this book enlightening and empowering.

Mary Ann Echols, Ph.D.

INTRODUCTION

Have you ever felt like your heart has been broken into a million and one pieces? Have you ever been so devastated and broken that you never thought you'd ever recover from the unexpected, devastating blows of life? A broken heart can occur at any time because of traumatic events in your life which creates pain and suffering. I should have been living on the back ward of the Ypsilanti State Mental Hospital forty years ago, But God who is rich and mercy delivered me.

I am so grateful to God for improving the quality and longevity of my life when He summoned me from Michigan to Ohio, instructed me to bring all the broken pieces of my heart to Him and to write my story, this testimony, For His Glory. I learned four key principles: brokenness, restoration, transformation and wholeness that God revealed regarding Inner Healing while under the teachings of the late, Bishop Norman L. Wagner.

Broken to Be Made Whole, is a book of hope that is written as a simple, fast-paced, relevant, healing, autobiographical testimony on Inner Healing. It's written straight from the heart of God, to my heart and from my heart to yours. Whether some wounds were self-inflicted or the effects and breaches from well intentioned, human, conditional relationships; or wounds incurred from natural causes, deaths, losses, accidents, birth defects and illnesses, God can sanctify, cleanse and heal you from your broken heart.

The purpose of this revised book is to bring self-awareness of the need for Inner Healing and deliverance and help others discover the areas in their lives where Inner Healing is needed. After being broken from blockages and receiving restoration, cleansing, Inner Healing and deliverance, it's imperative to develop the skills to maintain and sustain your healing. Living a transformative lifestyle leads to wholeness. The book is divide into four sections: Wounds, Worth, Work and

Wholeness. You will learn principles for Inner Healing, Mental Health, Wholeness and Biblical Healing as I share with you excerpts from some of my secular counseling and Biblical counseling sessions. My original testimony is still available in other versions, but is slightly abbreviated in this version to include more chapters, tools and lessons to promote self-awareness and participation during this healing process.

God used Broken to Be Made Whole in its original version, as one of the textbooks at Apostolic Church of God, pastored by the late Arthur M. Brazier, for their Recovery and Restoration Department for a number of years. I will always be grateful to the leadership and support from the Apostolic Church of God now pastored by his son, Dr. Byron T. Brazier and many churches in our organization, The Pentecostal Assemblies of the World, as well as other organizations and denominations who have supported me.

God anointed me as a church leader who could motivate and counsel others, win souls to the Lord, intercede for others, but, forgot about myself. I thought that I was being a true selfless, humble servant leader, until my friend, Evangelist Mary Green challenged me.

She said, "Girlfriend, you've used the books to help thousands of people heal and get saved. Now, why don't you read your own books and let God heal you? You wrote them, but you never took the time to read them for yourself and heal. Physician heal thyself. You referred many of us to Dr. Mary Ann Echols when our crisis was beyond your counseling ability, why don't you make an appointment for counseling with her for yourself? You can't counsel yourself." I thank God for my gifted, anointed, therapist, Dr. Mary Ann Echols, who is patiently, yet firmly walking me through my emotional healing process and holds me responsible as my accountability partner. Everyone needs friends that will speak the truth in love.

During the worldwide Covid19 Coronavirus Pandemic, while we were a nation that was shut in, I accepted Mary's challenge in 2020, the acceptable year of the Lord. What a difference this self-awareness and self-acceptance made before and during our 21 day spiritual detox led by my pastor, Sfg. Bishop C. Shawn Tyson. I became, "woke" as the young people say today. Pastor Tyson recently revealed that during the pandemic, God has us in isolation to prepare us on purpose for a purpose in 2021. God doesn't have us in isolation as a punishment, but is ushering the church and leadership into its finest hour as we prepare to be laborers for the massive harvest of souls in 2021.

Mental illness has always been an issue in the churches and we suffered in silence because of the stigma for decades. Yet, when I came to my breaking points, God was there every step of the way to give me breakthroughs, breaking me free from the wounds of the past.

Today, spiritual leaders are slowly recognizing that we are a trichotomy, spirit, soul and body, and the methods of Christian Disciplines, focusing solely on the spirit, have neglected to minister balance to the soul and body. I was elated after reading the article, "Let's Talk About Mental Health" by Bishop Roland E. Hairston in the magazine, The Christian Outlook. He shared, "Bishop Brooks believes that we can no longer ignore the "Elephant in the Room" that exists within our leadership and the larger church communities we serve……thus the theme: A Celebration of Wholeness – Building Bridges Together." I invite you to take a journey to wholeness through my life with me, to empower you as you reflect and reexamine your life. We all have a past history. Some of us are proud of our pasts, while it brings others of us shame.

As you read the 7th, newest edition of Broken to Be Made Whole, with new lens and a new perception of your personal wounds, look again, take one final look at your past; identify your worth and value, proceed to your purpose beyond your needs; begin writing in your journal to heal and never look back again. God will reveal your unconscious broken, childhood protective behavior patterns, the spiritual roots attached to the hidden patterns, and make you whole. The only time you will look back is to testify to others on how God brought you over unto the other side of brokenness, whole. We celebrate the love that God has given to us when we overcome by the blood of the lamb and the word of our testimonies. Please write, your Story to Give God Glory. Your story will help someone else heal.

SECTION ONE:
WOUNDS

CHAPTER 1
DON'T LET YOUR BACKGROUND KEEP YOUR BACK ON THE GROUND

As a child I felt like Humpty Dumpty who fell off the wall, broken into a million and one pieces. Life seemed to be filled with broken dreams and shattered visions. An egg like me is very sensitive, delicate and fragile, after all, and its contents are protected only by its outer shell. It's wrapped up so delicately that it requires nurturing and special care, otherwise, it will crack, then break. A crack developed in me very early, and I often wondered why God created me at all.

As I reflect back on my childhood, we were unaware of the affects that our childhood would have on our body, soul and spirit throughout our lives. Our parents had the best intentions and raised us with the generational skills and relationship patterns that they learned from their families. We survived. We enjoyed many privileges that working class/lower middle class children enjoyed and appeared to be a model family. Daddy had a very good paying factory job and was a good provider. Mama was a stay at home housewife and looked like the ideal wife and mother for years.

The five of us were clean, well-dressed, well-mannered and articulate.

Mama spent hours helping us with our homework, playing games, and building our vocabulary skills until people often complimented our parents on our proper speech and excellent grades. She also taught us our morals. She cooked homemade meals and baked all of her desserts from scratch. We would have to "call" for the cake pans, the beaters or the bowl as we ate the crumbs or licked the bowls. Oh, how we loved those times. We also loved to shop at Crowley's or J.L.Hudsons' department stores. Shopping, shopping, shopping!

Daddy was a lot of fun, he was humorous at times. He sat at the head of the dinner table and led the daily discussions. He gave us horsey back rides, took us on picnics, long Sunday drives and vacations. We had fun as we played hide and seek, and baseball in the middle of our street. Daddy wanted us to excel both athletically and academically so he taught us how to swim, bowl, golf, play tennis, ice skate and box. I also took piano, tap and ballet lessons. He exposed us to many social activities and political organizations. He wanted us to be tough and well-rounded. Daddy was brilliant and highly intelligent and we were outstanding students. He demanded perfection. You never had to guess what he felt. He said what he meant and meant what he said. He controlled the family. His attitude in life was reflected by his saying, "WHATEVER, I'm not always right, but I'm never wrong."

I didn't realize that shopping was Mama's coping mechanism for dealing with domestic violence. I call it retail therapy. The onset began in the womb.

CHILDHOOD SHELL

Who says that babies can't feel the pain and trauma while they are in their mother's womb? Studies indicate that as a fetus grows inside the mother's belly it can hear sounds from the outside world, understand them well enough to retain them after birth. The unborn baby or fetus sound processing part of the brain becomes active in the last trimester of their development. Sounds become extremely important in the mental well-being or mental distress.

I was their oldest child. Being born the oldest of five had great advantages and disadvantages. Most of the time I was responsible for finding safety for my siblings during my father's temper tantrums and outbursts. My father could make us all walk on eggshells and quake trembling with fear. One night I remember hearing screaming, yelling, sobbing and arguing. As the four of us ran downstairs into the den, we stopped at the door. Frozen in our tracks, we yelled, "Daddy, stop it!"

He shouted, "Shut up!" While my sister and brothers cried, I had to remain calm, I'm the *oldest.* I thought. I've got to do something to stop the fight. But what? I felt both helpless and responsible. I must really be a bad girl because they are fighting all of the time. Maybe if I am a good girl they will not fight.

I became my mother's counselor and comforter at a young age. She said, "Your father is a good man and a good provider. He just has this bad temper."

We watched Daddy choke and shove Mama into the wall for years, and we decided that the best way to settle arguments is to fight. We fought one another and others until sometimes the kids in the neighborhood had to go to the hospital. Daddy told us, "If someone starts a fight, you'd better finish it. Otherwise you'll have two whippings, one from them and one from me."

Even though I was the oldest, I remember feeling different. As my siblings were born they were much lighter than I was. Daddy questioned Mama about the differences in our colors when he told her, “You don’t put Black and Black together and come out with white, light and brown babies, look at how black Cheryl is.” “Sticks and stones may break my bones, but words will never hurt me”, was a Big Lie. I can still hear the echoes in my mind, “You’re the blackest in the family. You were born black!” I could see the difference in my complexion from my mother and siblings and felt the reactions of others who were color struck. I felt like the Black sheep!

I scrubbed my face every day, trying to wash the black off my skin, but I was still darker than everyone else except Daddy. I believed at that time if my complexion was lighter that I’d be accepted, until I understood they were called names such as yellow banana, Oreo cookie and other names and felt just as rejected as I did.

I was so tall with skinny legs and Mama said, “Your father told me to work with you and teach you how to walk straight because you are tall and thin, and he knows what such ridicule feels like." So Mama would hit me in my back and tell me, “Straighten up, and walk tall.” Okay, so now I get beat in my back every day.

In our neighborhood, on the Northeast side of Detroit, Michigan, we saw the same dysfunctional relationship pattern that we saw at home. Children learned what they saw in their environment, not what parents or adults say. While we were sitting on the front porch, I remember seeing Miss Pauline hit her husband, Mr. John, on the head, and knocking him out on the lawn every day. He'd lay there drunk for hours. But then he'd get up and beat Miss Pauline.

I saw Mr. Ivy chase Mrs. Ivy down the street with a gun. Every day I saw a young teenage mother of two toddlers follow her pimp husband, begging him to come back home.

I watched Mama wait on Daddy hand and foot, and yet, I wanted to be just like her and all the other women in the neighborhood. I thought that when you were married you had to cry a lot, and do everything men wanted you to do. I decided that I was going to be a good wife just like my Mama.

We developed into full blown perfectionist and the males learned that being right was more important than right relationships and the females learned pleasing men and relationships was more important than having rights, at any costs.

Yet, in the midst of all this, we were confused about healthy relationships and what true love was all about because we felt both love and fear. Daddy showed us love, I was even a Daddy's girl, but it seemed to me like he hated Mama, women, or something. I was mixed up! Daddy came home one day, plunked down at the kitchen table with a long, sad look on his face. He announced, "I lost my job. The plant closed down. I have an offer for another one in Los Angeles, California. I'll send for you as soon as possible." Even though our parents fought, we loved them and didn't want Daddy to leave.

I thought, "Daddy, how can you leave me? How could you? Not now! He was the only male in my life who validated my self-worth. He bought me beautiful clothes. He was the only man in my life who felt that I was attractive. Not now, Daddy, I thought not while it is so important to learn how to interact with the opposite sex and discover my identity."

The father-daughter relationship can have a huge impact on a young girl's life and even determine whether or not she develops into a strong, confident woman. A father's influence in his daughter's life helps to shape her identity. Her healthy interaction develops her self-image, confidence and opinions of men.

Feeling abandoned, the months turned into one year. It was rumored that Daddy really did leave us and never intended to send for us to move to California. Mama was overwhelmed with her new responsibilities and the drastic financial reversals. I remember those silver colored aluminum cans that the government commodities spam and peanut butter were in. I really liked the government cheese and butter.

The spirit of fear often took hold of her and she spent many days depressed, taking nerve pills and emotionally exhausted, sleeping on the sofa. We had two good intentioned parents, but they were both emotionally absent. We didn't have any aunts, uncles, grandmothers, or neighbors to model different choices other than abuse, fighting and pain. Nobody helped us to understand healthy family relationships. Domestic violence and abuse were our frame of reference until I visited my childhood friends, Evelyn, Eula, Pat, Claudette, LaVonia and eventually Regina, and Sherlyn often for a break. My friends' homes became my "safe places" and my godmother, Mama Taylor.

Our home was a safe place when Mrs. Cranford was our babysitter. She was a sanctified, Holy Ghost filled lady that wore these unusually thick stockings, long skirts and wore her hair in a bun on top of her head. She was an older, kind, compassionate, praying woman and my sister attended her Bible-Class every Saturday. God will never leave you nor forsake you. I believe schools need a spirit-filled grandparents' room!

In spite of the material provisions and financial comforts of home, the fights caused brokenness, great frustrations, insecurities, guilt and fears. I felt not only like a cracked and broken egg, but felt all scrambled up inside. Guilt is one of the major reasons for emotional problems. I thought it was my responsibility to stop the fights in the home. As a result, I'd suffered the first real crack in my shell. Guilt is a product of discouragement. I always felt that I had done something wrong or needed to take the blame for everything.

THE REJECTED – BULLIED SHELL

When Daddy left for California, I was afraid and felt unprotected I was bullied as I walked home from elementary school. The turmoil at home and fights in elementary school were minor compared to the endless ridicule, teasing and jeering I experienced at Cleveland Junior High School. The three-and-one-half-mile walk from junior high school, seemed like an endless, dangerous journey, as the boys continued to jeer, "Skinny legs, skinny legs, ha ha ha."

Cleveland, a very rough school at that time, had a bad reputation for fighting and stabbing. I was afraid and thought I might get stabbed and die if I had to keep on fighting. But I always remembered what Daddy said, "You'll get two whippings." My closest friends, Evelyn and Claudette lived on the next street. When their street was redlined or re-zoned that year, they had to attend Nolan Junior High School, and I didn't have anyone to walk home from school with. I believe my brother, Butch, walked his girlfriend home.

"I remember running home and playing my favorite song, "You'll Never Walk Alone" by Rogers and Hammerstein on the piano daily. The words of the song were combating the storms of life, comforting and encouraging me not to be afraid.

It begins with:

"When you walk through a storm, hold your head up high
And don't be afraid of the dark. For at the end of the storm is a golden sky
And the sweet silver song of a lark. Chorus: Walk on through the wind
Walk on through the rain though your dreams be tossed and blown
Walk on, walk on with hope in your heart and you'll never walk alone……"

God was with me through the bullying and bad times. He Will Never Leave You Nor Forsake You. Can you think of a song that can walk you through your storms in life? The right songs with the right sound that have meaning and purpose can anchor your soul and heal you. Attending school provided no protective shell, even though my grades were excellent. I developed a pleasing personality and outstanding grades as a facade to mask my real pain, anger and rage. I laughed to keep from crying even though I was crying on the inside.

Rejection, being left out, singled out, thrown aside, being ignored and feeling invisible is an excruciating, indescribable wound and pain that breaks your heart into a million and one pieces. Rejection leads to brokenness, which in Hebrew, "Shabar" means to be broken in pieces, to be torn violently or shattered, to sliver, to shatter, or to reduce to fragments; to fracture, ruptured; not properly functioning; out of order and splintered. It also means the mental anguish that comes from a devastating psychological blow. The implication is that something has been damaged beyond the hope of repair. Something is so damaged that nothing can be done. It means shattered, even crippled or maimed.

Harsh words causes rejection and brokenness that wound and kill more people than guns. People in the cliques would never understand the torment and pain. If they did, they'd stop it and become a committee of one to end bullying and discrimination. Bullying defined is when someone seeks to harm, intimidate, or coerce someone they perceive is vulnerable. Dr. Daniel Amen states, "Bullying puts kids at an increased risks of depression and anxiety disorders, not only during childhood and adolescence when the bullying occurs, but also long after the victimization stops. Bullying changes brain structure, and raises mental health risks."

I literally experienced three of the four types of bullying that are listed which are: (1) Physical bullying (2) Verbal bullying (3) Social bullying. I didn't experience the (4th) Cyberbullying because Facebook and other social media didn't exist then.

The signs and symptoms are: Increased moodiness, injuries they can't explain, social isolation, not wanting to go to school, avoiding using the restroom at school, changes in eating habits, trouble sleeping, a sudden drop in academic performance, frequent headaches and stomachaches, and faking illnesses to avoid going to school.

Tell your parents, tell a teacher, tell a friend, tell your pastor, tell a counselor, tell somebody who cares when you are being bullied and don't stop until someone listens and does something to help you. Develop a 1-800 Stop Bullying Hotline.

Social events were even more painful. Shaking and crying, I cried on the inside, "What's wrong with me?" At dances, I towered at least six to eight inches over the boys like a giraffe. No one asked me to dance. I was a wall flower, even though I was a good dancer. The only time I danced was when my childhood friend, Ernest said, "Cheryl, let's show them how to dance."

Rejection became a broken childhood pattern that prevented me from seeing myself whole. My wounds prohibited healthy and proper interactions in some relationships. Just because some people rejected me, didn't mean everyone rejected me. Others loved me in spite of how I felt about myself. Thank God.

ADOLESCENT SHELL

The girls in junior high gave me moral support. Being elected captain of the girls' junior high softball and basketball team, Vice President of the National Honor Society, Attendance Clerk, and nominated for class president increased my self-worth, or so I thought it did. By the time I reached high school, I'd become popular. The boys sought me to help them in their campaigns. David said, "If you want to win your election, get Cheryl to help you. She's really sweet and smart." I'd become like a sister to the boys.

I maintained a 3.5 - 4.0 grade point average. Life was exciting! With Daddy returning home, the family stable, and an improved social life, participating in roller skating, bowling and golfing, my recreation was not limited to parties only. I felt better about myself. But I still wanted bigger legs.

Driving one night to a ballet lesson, I was excited at the thought of developing "Big Legs," when crash, a drunken driver hit the rear of the car. I suffered from severe back and neck injuries from a whiplash for decades. The accident ended my ability to continue the dance classes.

Turning to roller skating to develop "Big Legs," I fell one night, at the Arcadia Roller Rink and was kicked in the head with steel skates and rushed to the Emergency Room of Detroit Receiving Hospital. I remember coming to and asking, "What in the world happened? How did I get here? My parents looked worried. The thought finally came to me, it's not really worth trying to have big legs! Forget it! My friends Evelyn, Claudette and eventually Sherlyn and I, continued to skate for recreation for years.

Becoming more comfortable with myself increased my continued popularity. Our family began attending the Methodist Church and not only appeared happy, but there were less fights in our home.

At sixteen, as a high school junior, life was great. Then Daddy came home with another announcement, "We will be moving from the northeast to the northwest side of town. Until the new house is ready, we'll move a few blocks from Cleveland Junior High for a few months." My new-found joy shattered. I was overwhelmed with the horrifying memories that flashed before my eyes of Cleveland Junior High. Old familiar words were repeated, "Skinny legs." Old feelings of self - hatred returned as I rode the bus to Pershing High School with those same boys. I was afraid to get on the bus in the morning and get off of it in the afternoon because of the teasing. The situation was painful. I cried every day for the four months until we moved into our new home. I thought, finally I thought that everything is going to be alright.

When perception is stronger than truth it leads to deception, victimization and intimidation.

My broken perception of myself, anxiety and fear of rejection, kept me from appreciating Daddy's desire to provide a better environment and education for his family. The social class system at Mumford High School was extremely upper or lower class and the middle class were mostly entertainers back then. We actually moved on the same street (Sorrento) that the late Aretha Franklin lived on. I have been in her foyer. As 16 year old teenagers, my friend and I waited until the late

Marvin Gaye's wife left home on Appoline, rang his doorbell and to our surprise, he invited us in. He showed us his albums from his performances at the Apollo Theater and his wall to wall stereo system. We enjoyed our brief visit and thanked him for his kindness.

We saw Barry Gordy's father on his front lawn at the corner of Meyers and Outer Drive, and many of the Motown entertainers such as, The Temptations and Miracles, because we lived in the same Outer Drive neighborhood in Northwest Detroit, Michigan. In spite of living in the midst of famous, wealthy, or highly educated African American role models, it was difficult for me to fit in.

I begged, "Daddy, please let go back to Pershing High School. I don't like Mumford. I don't belong here. Either you have to wear leather coats and be in the two gangs or your father has to be light-skinned, a doctor, lawyer or Jewish or an entertainer. You're none of these, so I don't fit. I can drive across town every day or catch the bus."

He said, "No! If I let you go back to Pershing, then your sister and brothers will want to return to their schools. That's just too much trouble!"

I found life was dull, gloomy and boring. School had lost its meaning. Nothing made me happy. I felt like a cloud was hovering over the top of my head and a one-hundred pound weight was crushing my shoulders. Sweaty palms, dizzy spells, and lumps in my throat were common daily symptoms. I lost my appetite, scraped most food into the garbage can, skipped lunch and existed on a steady diet of jelly beans and potato chips for years. About one hundred thoughts per second zoomed through my head. I felt crazy, like I wasn't myself. I developed an eating disorder, anorexia, self-inflicted wounds based upon my self-hatred. I was acting out my pain.

The truth was, I really never experienced rejection at Mumford High School. I actually benefited from my new environment. I was impacted by the successful role models and Jewish religious beliefs that I learned from classmates and co-workers. I continued to recite, "You shall be my people and I shall be your God" for grace every evening at the dinner table. I didn't know where the scripture was found in the Bible, nor what it really meant. I was literally prophesying my own future daily and totally unaware of the impact and difference this would make in my life one day. I was interjecting a new sound daily at the dinner table that "saved" my life, literally.

A series of blackouts began. One day, while on break as a cashier at a local grocery store, I blacked out on the counter. When I regained consciousness, I was in an emergency room!

"What happened? How did I get here?" I asked, not able to remember anything.

In a clothing store in downtown Detroit, while I stood making a purchase, I simply blacked out on the floor. Another day, standing at a teller's cage as I was cashing my paycheck, I came to looking into the face of a police officer standing over me. He handed me my money while I was sitting in a chair.

My grades began to suffer. For the first time I began receiving D's as a senior. The years in college at Eastern Michigan University in Ypsilanti, Michigan were a continuation of the downward trend at Mumford High School. My eating disorder caused hypoglycemia and I experienced blackouts on campus. While sitting in the cafeteria with friends, suddenly my brain felt like there was a vice or heavy grip on it. It felt like someone else was turning it tighter and tighter as bizarre thoughts of death, suicide and greatly exaggerated fears raced through my mind. The tears started and I began crying uncontrollably. Each time I was rushed off to the Emergency Room of the local hospital or the student health center, a regular place of rest. The doctors said I was experiencing growing pains.

At parties, I didn't have any emotional energy and stayed fatigued. I fell asleep in the middle of the dancing, and then slipped into an unconscious state. My grades were getting worse and eventually I flunked out of the university. Totally devastated, I packed my clothes as I heard classmates gossip about who had flunked out. They didn't realize that I had joined the failure list.

Upon my return to Detroit I secured employment at a downtown warehouse, where I met two very handsome young men. One was a son of an Apostolic Pentecostal preacher, and the other was from the South. Shocked that both were interested in me, I made a poor choice. I never chose the person that was good to me because they appeared dull, boring and uninteresting. They didn't seem to need me. I always chose the man that was flashy, fast-talking and handsome. I felt if they were good-looking they could help hide the ugliness that I felt about myself. But, Grandpa, who was a man about town, himself, used to always warn me about these type of men.

I never felt like I deserved anybody who was nice. I attracted bad boys.

Dating Benny, the young man from Decatur, Alabama, was consistent with my other poor choices in men. I was trying to find love in unhealthy relationships. I was actually wearing the wounds of a victim on my face that automatically attracted several immature men.

Childhood is very significant because we can trace the original causes and the effects of people practicing broken relationship patterns living in a broken world. Lack of self-worth, self-hatred and guilt are very damaging to a child's development and is caused by a lack of nurturing in childhood. A baby is just as fragile and delicate as an egg that must receive adequate light, sunshine, warmth and the right surroundings during its incubation period to develop without a crack or being broken.

Children can receive their basic needs and survive childhood. Christian families can provide good Christian morals, values, finances and their best intention for their children and still neglect meeting their emotional needs. If children have unmet needs, and do not feel or perceive their world as safe, during the formative years, their ability to cope in later years will be impaired by fear, anxiety, guilt, depression and sometimes suicide. My perception of life was distorted. When children live in any abusive environment (abnormal misuse of God's creation), Adverse Childhood Experiences interferes with their normal development, and it alters who they were created to be. When there is a vacuum in families children grow up to be angry and show off in temper tantrums. Angry teen-agers who have been ignored, ridiculed and have a warped sense of significance may succumb to peer-pressure and become a gang member, participate in criminal activity, or drugs or live their lives as victims. Dr. Tim Clinton and Dr, Gary Sibcy identify these vacuums as soul wounds. A soul wound is an emotional or relational attachment injury or wound that occurs when in times of stress we expected a loved one to be there for us and for whatever reason there were unavailable. There are four attachment styles:

1. Secure – Feel worthy of love and capable of giving and receiving love.
2. Ambivalent – Feel unworthy and not capable of receiving love
3. Avoidant – Feel worthy of love but don't trust others to give love
4. Disorganized – Feels unworthy of love and not capable of receiving because others are abusive.

Today, mental health problems that affects a person's thinking, emotional state, and behavior are diagnosable illnesses often rooted in soul wounds. **Mental illness is defined as a condition affecting thinking, perceptions, moods, emotions, and behaviors which diminish the quality and longevity of life.** Our nations' work force and military are at great risks if these illnesses disrupts the persons ability to work or carry out other daily activities and engage in satisfying personal relationships. ACE (Adverse Childhood Experiences) Resilience studies, the largest public health study, originated in 1985 in Dr. Vincent Felitti's obesity clinic in California.

In 1998 the Kaiser Permanente and the Centers for Disease Control Prevention uncovered a stunning link between childhood trauma and the chronic diseases people develop as adults, as well as mental, social and emotional problems. Dr. Felitti and Dr. Robert Anda developed a scoring system for ACEs. It identifies measurable types of trauma experienced in childhood as another cause of some illnesses and provides prevention and intervention services to young children as well as adults dealing with the effects, ACE Resilience.

Although most people associate Post -Traumatic Stress Disorder with soldiers in combat during wars, people who experience ACEs such as domestic violence as well as accidents, or are victims of crimes and natural disasters i.e. pandemics can experience the exact same symptoms.

Many veterans are treated for Post-Traumatic Stress Disorders (PTSD), anxiety triggered by a traumatic event, several years later, while many children who experienced warzones in their homes go undiagnosed and live with unhealthy, irrational thinking patterns, damaged emotions and inappropriate behavior patterns. They may be successful and survive for years before the flashbacks are triggered. I wasn't diagnosed with this chronic stress disorder until forty years later, during menopause.

When children grow up being controlled and receive well-intentioned conditional love and acceptance based on how well they perform; and aren't allowed any room for weakness or failure; in adulthood, unconscious stress-related issues will limit their ability to thrive, even though they appear to have it altogether. Often those who succeed in any profession or occupation, even ministry, still battle unconsciously with unresolved issues of the heart, a broken heart.

I wanted to be free from that scared, frightened little girl of my past. I wanted to be that person that I was created to be. But there was a big gap and I always wondered how to bridge the span between who I pretended to be, who others wanted me to be, and who I really was. Who am I? I wondered. I appeared paradoxical. A seemingly healthy, stable childhood with two well-meaning parents; a sister and three brothers by that time, who all excelled in school as well as myself; financially stable, and finally somewhat popular by the time I reached high school for a brief period of time. It seemed to be a good life, but I could not find the real me.

I remember an advisor at the Eastern Michigan University Career Center, taught me one principle that I never forgot: "You will never get to where you're going, if you don't know where you came from, where you are located now, and where you are going on this journey of life."

My first step to wholeness is that I must recognize my broken places and become self-aware of the broken generational childhood protective patterns that has caused lifetime challenges and brokenness, acknowledge it and refuse to let the effects of my background keep my back on the ground. Brokenness precedes wholeness. We were created to love and be successful individuals, dominating life in every aspect, spiritually, physically, emotionally, mentally, socially, financially and morally. Every one of us are given unique qualities and characteristics before we were born, because God created us for a specific purpose. We will always be successful when we fulfill what God has called and created us to do. "We will always be the first seed of the harvest you were created to reproduce." We were created to solve a problem or meet a need on earth, and therefore we are not biological accidents. We are given unique gifts to use for the sake of others. We are a solution to somebodies problem. This is the absolute, undeniable truth. God wants us to use our mind and think correctly and foster wholeness in the earth.

The Law of Original Intentions, what God really pre-designed for us in the beginning, explains that we were created to dominate the earth for God. God is not the blame for our brokenness, but, the sin nature of mankind causes brokenness, ACE's, soul wounds and bad things to happen to innocent and good people. Our Histories Are Not Our Destinies. Our challenging pasts was our preparation for our purposes. Remember, we are already loved and accepted by God before the foundation of the world. Our purpose in life is to learn to celebrate the love that God gave us. "Don't Let Your Background, Keep Your Back on the Ground!" Children of God are resilient because with new skills, divine revelations, information, strategies, help, hope and love, we can walk through and overcome any adversity in time once we recognize the truth and face the heart of the matter.

"Stop Looking For Love In All The Wrong Places."

CHAPTER 2
STOP LOOKING FOR LOVE IN ALL THE WRONG PLACES

THE ADULT SHELL

I continued my relentless search, desperately looking for love in all the wrong places, searching to fulfill unmet emotional needs in unhealthy ways. Soul wounds influence our choices.

"Will you marry me?" Here's the presence of that unloving spirit continuing to wreak havoc in our families for the next generations.

"Yes, I exclaimed! Finally somebody loved me! Benny was an extremely handsome man that had a very charming, likeable personality. He would light up a room when he entered it. He could mingle with everyone from the ghetto to the White House. He never met a stranger. He came from a large southern, supportive family that I absolutely loved and they loved me. We'd laugh until we cried and I experienced more risk taking adventures with him. Wow. I was flattered and honored that he would even look at me, ask me to marry him, who me?

My mother was threatening to put me out of the house because I was no longer performing household chores. "I'm sick, Mama, I don't know what's wrong, but it feels like I have a terminal disease or something. I don't have any energy after I come home from work. I sweat all the time, feel dizzy, have severe back and neck pains, blackouts and crying spells." I told her these things, but she classified them as nothing but "excuses." Mama, as well as many parents, caregivers and professionals were unfamiliar with the signs and symptoms of chronic clinical depression and anxiety at that time. Mental Health issues were and still can be misinterpreted as laziness, even though these symptoms are cries for help. Newsflash, be aware today.

The psychiatrist even misdiagnosed me and told me that my blackouts on campus were simply "growing pains", but I've had the same symptoms for two years. I felt like dying. I told Mama, "I have no energy for doing household chores. You'll see I won't be alive much longer, but Benny asked me to marry him. He understands my sickness." Mama said, "So you think that's going to solve your problems! He's a handsome, charming man, but your father and I agree he is not going to make you a good husband. Your daddy does not want to say much, but he is heartbroken. He told me that it will never work."

Benny's oldest sister also warned me, "He's not the marrying kind." His ex-wife and I talked before our marriage. She warned me." When I confronted him concerning their remarks, he laughed and said, "Oh, yeah, I didn't love my first wife. That's why my sister thinks I'm not ready, but I love you. I'm not going to do that to you." I believed him and thought that with lots of love, I could change him.

Two days before the wedding, our marriage license was delayed because his physical was questionable. When a person shows you who they are, believe them, don't try to fix them. In spite of all warnings, on September 21, 1968, I became Mrs. Benny Bass, Jr. That day I heard my mother say, "It will never work."

During the marriage we both received our pay checks every Friday. His contribution toward the household amounted to five dollars, forcing me to use my entire pay. He mailed his money to his step-father to help support his ten younger brothers and a sister, or so he said. While we were yet newlyweds, he sent for some of his brothers and a couple of his male friends to come and live with us. I cooked, cleaned and washed for all five males, while I worked and attended junior college full-time.

My business teacher commented, "Oh, Mrs. Bass, you are losing so much weight since you have been married, (I wore a size 1). Are you sick?" Smiling, I replied, "I'm fine." On the inside the response was, "Yes, I'm sick! Sick of this man! Sick of this mess! Help me!" Benny continued to womanize. Within five months of my marriage, I was back home. I decided to go for a checkup. I couldn't believe my ears when I heard, "You're pregnant." When I rushed home and told Daddy, he looked as though he had seen a ghost. He said, "You'd better get a good education because you're going to have to raise this child." Mama added, "We'll help you, but the responsibility is yours."

Frightened, I thought a baby might help Benny accept his own responsibilities. We discussed reconciling and Benny said, "Let me come get you next Saturday. This Saturday I'm going out of town."

"Okay."

Excited that we would be a family with a baby, I went downtown to shop when, who did I see, but this tall, light-skinned, six-foot three, handsome, thin man that looked just like my husband, escorting a tall, thin, brown-skinned woman. I walked up to them at Baker's Shoe Store in downtown Detroit and yelled, "So, Benny, this is how you spend your weekends out of town!"

I screamed, "Hello, you must be Loretta, you fit the description Benny gave me of you. You're all the way from Indiana, but you may as well go back home. I'm Benny Bass's wife, Cheryl."

Stunned, she looked at Benny first, then at me, and ran out of the store. Benny started after her, but I told him, "You better not move!" Taking a shoe from the display I began to beat him in his stomach and back until the shoe salesman kicked both of us out. There on the streets I continued hitting him with my fists and cried. I was an angry woman. He came and brought me back to our home, but he did not change. We continued to fight like cats and dogs. The verbal and emotional abuse continued and my unborn baby experienced the same arguing and fighting with disturbing sounds as I did. The sins of the fathers are visited upon the children for generations. Children often suffer for the bad things their parents do.

A couple of months after we reconciled he came home and announced, "I've just been drafted into the army." At a very crucial time, Benny was gone for almost four months. The Red Cross notified me at Grandpa's home where I was staying, that Benny was coming home on an emergency leave for the birth of his child. Five days after her birth he was deployed to Vietnam and was stationed there for thirteen months. Because of harboring so many fears and insecurities, I found out that entering motherhood without a husband at home was very challenging for me.

My family, friends, college mates and Benny's Aunt Sarah were great support systems. With thirteen paternal aunts and uncles and four maternal aunts and uncles not even counting their mates; three grand-parents, two godmothers and a hosts of others, Juanita LaShawn, "Shawnie" became a blessed child. People were not only drawn to her, but also to her father. Once during the tenth month of her father's tour in Vietnam, the government paid for us to meet him in Hawaii for his Rest and Recuperation. People complimented my husband and daughter on their fine looks. They flooded Shawnie with free souvenirs and commented how she and her daddy both looked like Hawaiians. She resembled her father with her beautiful caramel complexion and naturally soft, curly black hair.

When we returned home I was treated for an infection transmitted by Benny. You'd think by now, that was enough, but I waited for him to be discharged, believing he'd change. I gave him the benefit of the doubt, because the war movies I saw were horrific, and I commended anyone who returned home alive. Thank you for your service.

THE CO-DEPENDENT SHELL

When he returned home, his adjustment to civilian life was complicated by the fact that he'd become addicted to heroin. His progression from marijuana to heroin was a reality. I was a certified Co-Dependent, (lose yourself, love deficit disease) where I supported or enabled Benny's sexual addictions, poor mental health, immaturity, irresponsibility and drug abuse.

The night before he was discharged my friend, Cynthia, and I spent all night in the kitchen preparing his favorite meal, fried chicken, greens, chitterlings, macaroni and cheese, pinto beans and cornbread. When Shawnie and I picked him up from the airport, he had a friend, Eddie, who he wanted to bring home with him. Benny didn't even appreciate the meal. Drugs had become his first love, other women were his second love.

Since my family was very sensitive, it seemed as though the crisis that I was experiencing brought all of us closer together. The pain that I'd felt from being the Black sheep no longer existed.

They also began to express how they really felt. Denise said, "You have always been my role model. Because you received good grades, I wanted to get them too. When I was afraid to drive on the highway, I learned because I said, Cheryl is a good highway driver! When I enrolled at the University of Michigan in Ann Arbor, it was because they offered me a scholarship, but you were a few miles away at Eastern Michigan University. I even majored in Sociology because you majored in Sociology.

My middle brother, Darrell, took my daughter and me to the drive-in theater because Benny seldom spent time with us as a family. As we were leaving, a car cut in front of Darrell. By the time I said, "Watch out, you're going to hit ...." we had a terrible accident. I grabbed Shawnie, who was five months old, who was sitting on my lap, to keep her from being thrown through the windshield. I was thrown partially through the glass which required twenty-eight stitches in my face and several in my knee. Shawnie only needed five stitches to close the cut in her ear. Mama and Denise were there in no time. Denise told me, “Mama already knew something was going to happen to you tonight. When I arrived home from work, after midnight she told me to keep my coat on, I sense they’re in trouble and we’re going to rush to their aid.”

The hospital tried to contact Benny all night. The neighbors said they heard the telephone ring continuously until he came home and answered it around 4:00 a.m. He came to the hospital, looked at my face and said, "Oh, Cheryl, you're ruined for life." With that he walked out of the room. Devastated, I realized this abuse had to end. I overheard Mama saying, "We are going to eventually have to pay for plastic surgery because you know Cheryl already has a complex. Scars on her face won't help her at all."

I wondered, how do I look? I began to make plans to leave Benny. I'd had enough. He didn't even come home with the car to take me to the doctor to remove the stitches. I called my girlfriend, Sherlyn, to take me to the doctor as we had a long talk about the abuse. She was a social worker for abused foster children, and she told me, "Girl, you know I have seen so many abused children, but I've never seen anyone go through the abuse Benny's putting you through. If there is anything I can do to help you, I will. If you decide to stay with him, I just hope things will work out. I just want my goddaughter to be happy. Cheryl, you ought to write a book. Here!" She gave me a blank book called The Nothing Book. I will always be grateful to my friend, the late Detective Sergeant Sherlyn Fleming, who inspired me to write my life experiences in the Nothing Book. God took The Nothing Book and created it into Broken to Be Made Whole and gave meaning and purpose for my broken experiences. I decided to leave him that day.

Benny begged, "Cheryl, let's start our life all over again and move to Ypsilanti since you're in school and I am working there.

Realizing I have been guilty of perhaps the family knowing too much of our business, I felt he was right. Maybe somehow we could work it out. Guilt became the basis for many of my decisions. I always felt responsible for everything. We moved to Ypsilanti where I attended Eastern Michigan University. I'd been readmitted after flunking out. I'd improved my grade point to a 3.0 by attending Highland Park Community College for the past two years.

The college campus Family Housing Unit consisted of a majority of single female heads of household attending college. During this time Benny was like a kid in a candy store, moving from one woman to another.

I yelled, "I'll show you two can play this game, brother."

After that I started drinking and smoking marijuana and frequenting nightclubs, sometimes dancing all night long. One night my friend, Ellie, came by. We drank a bottle of Boones Farm Strawberry Hill wine and smoked marijuana before we went to Eastern Michigan Universities' basketball game. When we arrived there we were so drugged that we could barely sit on the bleachers. About half-time, I yelled to Ellie, "Look! There's that girl that slept with Benny! I'm going to kill her tonight!" Reaching in my purse, I took out a letter opener. As I stood up to run, I felt a hot rush to my head. I was so mad, I couldn't see straight. I was running down the bleachers with Ellie right after me.

I was just about to stab the girl's heart out, when I heard an inner voice say. "Don't ruin your life. She's not worth it."

I stopped, looked at Ellie, and shook my head. I looked at my friend again and yelled," What did you say?"

She screamed as she snatched me by my clothes, "Don't do it."

I asked her, "But did you say, "Don't ruin your life. She's not worth it?"

She said, "No!"

I looked around for the voice I'd heard and knew it wasn't Ellie's. The whole thing sobered me up. We left the game. I never saw her again.

The turning point came when he apologized and said, "Baby, I've got a new job with the government as a Federal Corrections Officer. "I told Ellie, "Benny promised no more women, drugs and abuse. We're going to start our marriage all over again." Excited, we left the sociology class and both got in our cars. When I reached in the backseat for my purse, my fingers found a strange object. A wallet! Puzzled, I slowly looked through it when I saw the license of another woman of another mother and another color. My heart sank. Tears flooded my face. "He lied again. It all makes sense," I cried.

THE BATTERED SHELLS

One night I noticed my car was missing. Benny insisted that he go alone to retrieve it. Was I really that naïve to believe everything that he said? No, I was in denial and I didn't want to take the responsibility when I admitted the truth to myself. I was calling evil good, hiding behind the marriage vows, for better or worse. I allowed myself to be victimized. He let this woman drive my car. He returned in an hour with both cars. That's it! This marriage is over! Get out of my life!"

Never denying that he lent her the car, he simply moved in with her. Hurt, angry and wounded, whenever we encountered one another in the small city, Benny and I engaged in physical fights on the streets. He beat my back and face with a deodorant can. He busted my lip. I yelled, "Why should you see your child when you are so low-down and you brag about quitting a government job to avoid paying child support? You say no man is going to make you pay child support. Then no man is going to make me let you visit your child!"

Finally, filing for a divorce, I found it was also necessary to file a restraining order.

The police officer told me, "There isn't too much we can do in domestic violence cases." It wasn't against the law at that time.

I asked, "What does it take to get some help, when they start beating you whenever they feel like it?"

He said, "There's not too much that can be done unless they really hurt you."

I replied, "Oh, so you have to be pretty near dead to get some help. Well, I'm going to shoot him, before he hurts me again."

He agreed, "That's what you have to do." I decided to get a life, but I didn't know how to change.

Graduating a few months later with a Bachelor's Degree, I thought, life will be better with a degree, a new job, boyfriend and money. I was wrong. Nothing eased the pain from a broken-heart when someone you thought would love you, didn't know how to love. How do you cover a broken-heart? Everything that I thought would help were nothing more than band aids. Yet, life goes on, broken-heart and all. I walked with a limp, or felt like the walking dead, there was no light nor life in my eyes. I resigned from my first job due to sexual harassment.

Then I was employed as a Basic Education Teacher in the Ann Arbor School System and loved my new occupation working in an alternative program for students with emotional problems. It was easy for me to relate to the pain of the students who were in dysfunctional relationships.

Attending modeling school part time to overcome inferiority and insecurity was challenging but exciting. Life seemed better. I traveled to Africa that April as a high school chaperone for The Black Studies Club. In flight, I met a young, tall, handsome millionaire who swept me off my feet. Our high school counselor, Mr. Shag Johnson, introduced me to him.

He said, "Cheryl, this is Roy (fictitious name) and we've been searching for you all night on the plane, but you were asleep. Roy beamed, "Cheryl, the pleasure is mine. I understand you will be residing in Senegal for a few days. When you arrive in Accra, Ghana give me a call at my chalet, and I'll show you the city."

My eyes lit up and I smiled, took his number and agreed, "I will call you. Thank You." I couldn't wait until we arrived in Accra. Beginning to experience dizzy spells once again, I fainted and woke up in the local hospital. The doctor declared, "You had an allergic reaction to the malaria shot."

I called Roy after my discharge and he came to the dormitories where we were staying to pick me up. After a wonderful trip of a lifetime for eighteen days, I was greatly impacted by the sacrifices of the African slaves, their strength to endure cruelty, their intellect and their accomplishments and their genius. These strong men and women are our ancestors. I was empowered to live a life of purpose and significance. Africa is one of the most beautiful and breath-taking places I've ever visited. I was returning home saying, "I'm Black and I'm Proud." The beautiful, dark-skinned people greatly impacted my self-image in a positive way. I began to change my perception and embraced my God-given complexion.

Our return flight from Accra, Ghana to John F. Kennedy airport took ten hours and I was daydreaming and beaming the entire time. We boarded in New York and everyone was looking forward to the short forty-five minute flight returning home. I really missed Shawnie and my family. I was looking out of the window as we were descending and preparing for landing, and I saw orange and white emergency vehicles as we circled the Metropolitan Airport in Detroit, several times. Curious, I looked at the airline stewardess whose face was frozen with fear and before she could say anything, I knew that we were in danger.

Suddenly she squealed, "Return to your seats, put your seat belts on, take off your jewelry and shoes and place them in the bag. Assume the emergency landing position (place your head in your lap and clasp your legs with your hands). We are circling the airport to burn up some fuel because our landing gear is not working. If we crash we don't want any gas in the tank." All I could think of is, I won't ever see my three-year old daughter again, my mother, my father. The students started yelling and screaming and crying and I told them to be still, stop yelling and screaming, it's not going to help, calm down. This was the eeriest feeling, with my head in my lap, we descended for a possible landing, I remember saying, "If we live, we live, and if we die, we die, there's nothing we can do now. I didn't have enough sense to pray.

When the plane made a harsh, bumpy landing, I cried like a baby, and was relieved with sheer joy and unbelief. I still didn't know God, but I realized that for some reason I was being kept alive for a purpose. What my purpose and destiny is, I'm not sure. But, I was determined to discover why I'm still alive. I could hear echoes of the same soft, still voice, "You are my people and I am your God." Without a vision (purpose) the people perish. We were spared for a reason, a purpose.

Roy invited me to visit him in the states during the summer vacation. When I arrived at the Los Angeles airport, his chauffeur drove me to his home in the mountains of Altadena, California. ! I was highly impressed with him having a chauffeur, a beautiful home, and everything.

My relief was short-lived as I noticed the type of people that came to the house. Drug dealers, pimps, prostitutes, you-name-it, they were there. Just like the movies. I learned that Roy was also starring as a pimp in a major motion picture.

I groaned, Oh no, Roy is a hustler, and a drug dealer and a pimp. Roy ordered, "Go upstairs. Change your clothes for the party. It's going to start at 4 o'clock in the afternoon." Initially I became fearful and stunned, I froze in my tracks. Immediately I was angry.

He hollered, "You move when I tell you! I've thrown people over my patio, down the side of this mountain and they've never been found! I will do that to you too! I want you to greet the guests. Do as I tell you and we will get along fine." I never changed clothes because I can't stand to hear people yelling at me or anybody; I became defiant and combative or passive-aggressive with controlling men. I dared him to even try it!

I encountered my first experience with cocaine, hash and angel dust. My head started to spin, I asked, "What in the world is this?" As the group laughed, it felt like my mind left my head, moved to the left, returned, and moved to the right and kept on going. They yelled, "Angel dust!"

That drug is an animal tranquilizer that arrived on the West Coast years before it was used as a drug in the Midwest. After using angel dust, people often die as a result of the psychotic reaction they experience. They think they now have the strength of superman and actually try to stop trains on tracks or fly. Others have been admitted to backwards of mental institutions because of the immediate loss of contact with reality following a psychotic break. I continued such action for four days.

Finally, when Roy left the house, I heard the same voice that spoke to me for years speak, "Call Michelle Cochrane."

God reminded me that Daddy lived with the Cochrane family twelve years ago in Los Angeles, when I was twelve. Their oldest daughter Mickey, and I were the same age and we had been pen pals for years.

In desperation, I searched for the city telephone directory, located it and found the phone number. "Oh, Lord, please let someone be home."

The phone rang. After what seemed like an eternity, I heard a voice say, "Hello." That word never sounded so good in my entire life. "Is this the Cochrane residence?"

"Yes, it is."

"Is Michelle home?"

"This is she."

"Oh, Mickey, this is Cheryl Nelson and I'm in the Los Angeles area and need your help."

After explaining all of the circumstances, she took the address, described her car, and said, "Cheryl, I'm on my way to get you. It'll take me an hour." I will always be grateful to Mickey, I just wish that I could find her.

Relieved, I hung up and cried for joy. In the meantime, after calling Mickey, I hurried through the house and began packing. In the midst of this, Roy returned home before she arrived.

Running past him without my belongings, I yelled, "I can't live like this! Please let me go! Keep my clothes, just let me go!"

He answered calmly, "Okay, Baby, take good care of yourself, I hope you get yourself together soon." I thought that I had problems and was weird, but I had more going for me than I realized. You are the ones that need help." Everyone has issues, no one is exempt.

The hour before Mickey came seemed to drag on forever. My, she was a sight for sore eyes! As Mickey and I hugged, Roy brought my clothes to the car. Once he put them inside, he kissed me and said, "Give me a call sometime and let me know how you are."

I looked at him, smiled and sat back in that Toyota. While we rode down the mountain side, Mickey and I laughed and cried as I told her some of the things that happened.

Spending the rest of the nine days with her brought a refreshing change. They took me to Disneyland, on a picnic, shopping and boating.

There are no coincidences, I felt rejected when my father lived in California when I was twelve years old, but it was a set-up for my safety and divine protection.

MY PERCEIVED REJECTION WAS PROTECTION

Daddy, in God's divine plan, was sent to California twelve years before I encountered a traumatic crisis to provide a contact person. The only person I'd ever known and had contact with in the entire state of California, at that time. What a God! He will never leave you nor forsake you. Way to go Daddy.

Upon my return to Michigan, I experienced bad memory lapses, mood swings and an evident personality change from the drug abuse. I've never had a good memory since that trip, I suffered some slight brain damage.

Still looking for love, I spent the rest of the summer with my brother, Butch and his family who was stationed on the army base in Colorado Springs, Colorado. I met a very handsome man and was unaware that he and his estranged common-law wife were trying to reconcile. Tommy (fictitious) and I made plans to go roller skating in Denver. While talking outside of his apartment complex, Tommy pushed me back into the brick building. After cursing him out, I yelled, "What's the matter with you?"

At that moment I saw his wife with a glistening butcher knife in her hand. As he wrestled and tried to reason with her, I was angry and panicked, as I took the Boones Farm Strawberry Hill wine bottle out of the bag, grabbed it as a weapon and proceeded to hit her on her temple and follow through at the eyes. At that moment, the same voice I heard as a college senior, warned, "Why destroy your whole life? Don't kill her. I'll give you a love of your own. I love you." That was now the third or fourth time that comforting voice spoke to me. I left Tommy and his wife there arguing and returned to Butch's apartment. He asked, "What happened? Why aren't you going skating?"

I told him, "It's okay, just a few problems, but I keep hearing this voice talking to me." He gave me a puzzled look as I went to my room. Within a few days Daddy drove my mother, my siblings Denise, Darrell and Rex, and my daughter Shawnie to Colorado from Michigan for a vacation. Heartbroken, I flew home alone to Michigan with another crack in the shell. Shortly after that, my ex-husband called. Benny declared, "I just reenlisted in the army. I'm mature now and I want us to get married again."

I said, "Benny, please don't hurt us. If you don't mean us any good, don't come up here. I'm sick, hurt and can't take too much more. I can't take another heartbreak."

He answered, "Oh, no, Cheryl. I learned my lesson. Since I've matured I'll become a better husband and a better father to Shawnie. You'll see." He came and moved us to Ft. Hood Army Base in Killeen, Texas.

THE MENTALLY CHALLENGED SHELL

Before we could remarry, strange events occurred. He fell asleep at the stop light in traffic. I yelled, "Benny, wake up! You are going to get us killed! What's wrong with you?" He drove by his sergeant's house daily, left us in the car, stayed ten minutes, and nodded off the rest of the day. One day he stayed too long. Shawnie and I waited in the car for forty minutes, only to discover he had overdosed and they were shooting his system with salt to neutralize the effects of too many drugs. I drove us home and he slept for twenty-four hours after that experience. All types of strange people came to our house. By that time, my nerves were frazzled. One night I grabbed his gun and yelled, "If another person comes here, I'll shoot you and them."

On Shawnie's fifth birthday, Benny said he left to get her a cake and ice cream. After we waited for several hours, Shawnie and I walked at night on the army base to buy her a cupcake, since I only had twenty-five cents. When we got back, I placed a match in it and lit it, then sang happy birthday. She seemed to enjoy her little cake. On other occasions we ate lettuce with French dressing for dinner. All his pay had disappeared. We were destitute. The army eventually court martialed Benny and ordered him into a Drug Rehabilitation Halfway House. He lost his rank and his pay.

I secured a job at Ft. Hood’s Educational Center, teaching GI's the Basic Education Skills. That brief experience was very rewarding. The men excelled in the six week cycles by at least two reading levels. Many passed their GED exams and were able to remain in the Army.

While Benny was in the halfway house, I attended individual and group counseling. In the private sessions the psychologist stated, "You are a doormat and you have allowed people to walk all over you without taking control of your life. Set new boundaries and detach with love. You demonstrate no self-love, worth, or esteem, so build up your self-worth. It will take your husband a life time to learn to love himself. That means he will never learn to love you or your daughter.

"He is a very self-centered narcissist, and immature man and you will never be able to change, nor please him no matter how hard you try. It'll never work. In our profession we provide hope for potential restoration, but you will destroy yourself if you remain with him. He has and will only bring you pain.

"You must learn to love yourself and your daughter. You learned depression from your childhood and emulated your mother, and have a passive-aggressive personality. You've experienced so much abuse, that you are immune to it, and cannot feel pain or any emotions. You are also suffering from chronic clinical depression and anxiety neurosis. Those blackouts are anxiety attacks which shut down your entire system when you are faced with conflicts.

"Your treatment plan will include assisting you in decision making and goal-setting in your present dilemma and you will need the support of a group to give you feedback and love. You are starved for love and very lonely."

What is depression? The American Heritage Dictionary defines it as the condition of anyone who is low in spirits, sad or has feelings of despondency or dejection. Depression is also anger turned inward. Depression is a mood disorder. The Dictionary of Bible Themes, 5831 defines depression as a deep sense of despondency, discouragement and sadness, often linked with a sense of personal powerlessness and a loss of meaning in and enthusiasm for life.

There are external, physical illness and internal causes for depression. The depression caused by external circumstances is by something real, something going on in your life such as a sudden death of a loved one, financial problems, physical challenges, and where "life happens." Almost everyone experiences depression at one time or another and feel sad or have the blues due to human experiences. This type of depression is acute, short lived and solely based on life's circumstances or situations.

The internal causes of depression can result as long-term sadness from a devastating psychological blow. Because this condition exists for a longer period of time, it often disrupts your entire body, soul and spirit causing a chemical imbalance, the lack of serotonin in the brain. A broken hearted person, when wallowing in the pain can become chronically and clinical depressed, which is classified as a mental illness.

The internal causes of depression is maintained by the negative thinking about the external events due to years of automatic negative thoughts (ants). These automatic thoughts are a result of habits from past events and negative thinking. These negative thoughts bring on stress symptoms such as indecision, frustration, bewilderment, loneliness, fears, loss of sense of God's presence, feeling forsaken by God, etc. and internal echoes such as, "What's wrong with me? Why does this happen to me? Nothing ever goes right for me. I'm so stupid." These are not valid thoughts because they are not true. They are negative thoughts. When your body is continually bombarded with negative thoughts it begins to increase physical symptoms.

The church leaders must learn how to make a distinction between the external and internal causes of depression, then minister accordingly without rebuking a demon even if their depression is a sinful reaction to unhealthy, abusive relationships. The minister must exercise wisdom and counteract their internal dialogue and sounds with the question, "What happened to you?" and not

"What's wrong with you?" The skilled counseling agent will use a positive approach of "possibility" rather than labels and "pathology". Healing from internal depression requires love.

Twenty percent of mental illness in general are disorders of the brain, your body's most important organ. It is a disease, much like heart disease or cancer or the result of an injury. It's no one's fault, not the family, nor the person's. There are many physical causes for depression such as birth trauma, chemical imbalances in the brain, where there is a lack of serotonin in the brain, heredity, stress and other biological, environmental, social and cultural factors.

Regardless of the causes the symptoms are similar. These persons generate persistent sadness and a sense of hopelessness. These people live with feelings of self-hatred and low self-worth, reducing their ability to perform to their full potential. They appear mean to others, but they are irritable and prefer to isolate themselves. This type of depression requires time, prayer, support, and in some cases, counseling and sometimes, temporary medication, until the client, such as myself, becomes stable, focused and able to understand and apply the spiritual principles for healing.

Symptoms of Depression
Unusually sad mood, sad feelings
Loss of interest in enjoyable activities, withdraw and isolate
Lack of energy, fatigue, lethargy and tired
Feel worthless, hopeless, helpless, inadequate and guilty
Difficulty thinking, inability to concentrate, confusion, extreme emotional pain and difficulty making decisions and right choices
Irritable and easily agitated
Sleep disturbances, too much sleep, too little sleep
Appetite disturbances, overeating, poor appetite
May think about death and suicide and negative thoughts

During secular counseling, I was too numb to respond to anything. I had a difficult time expressing anger or any feelings. I cried through most of the sessions. While in the group, I was able to identify with a young girl who was discharged from the army because of anxiety attacks. For the first time I'd met someone else who could identify with my sickness. The sickness even had a name, anxiety. Anxiety is defined as fear, cares or on-going unrealistic, excessive worry, having unpleasant feelings or anxious thoughts; dread; expecting something unpleasant often unknown or uncertain; alarm (fight or flight). Fear is also defined as: to be startled, to be afraid or to make to shake. The Bible also states fear is a spirit. Neurological responses to fear produce shaking and trembling that come out of anxiety.

Symptoms of Anxiety

Mind racing thoughts
Decreased ability to concentrate
Confusion
Sleep disturbances
Nervous, restless feeling on edge
Anger
Indecisive
Impatient
Gastro-intestinal problems – digestion problems
Muscle aches
Inability to relax
Avoidance behaviors – distress in social situations

The root cause of anxiety can be a broken heart, insecurity and low self-esteem. Anxiety, like depression can be normal due to acute fear of something that is new or different, temporary illnesses and the unexpected such as this Covid19 coronavirus pandemic 2020. An anxiety disorder is a chronic and irrational fear that persist about the future without a cause. The body stays in a fight, flight or freeze stance, increasing adrenaline resulting in fatigue and nervous exhaustion. It's difficult to process information, to focus, concentrate and think.

Can you imagine living in this ball of confusion for years? Why not? You live with them, you see them, you work with them, you fellowship with them at church. In the United States, anxiety affects over 44 million adults who are 18 years old and older. Globally, an estimated 284 million people experienced anxiety disorder in 2017, making it the most prevalent mental health or neurodevelopmental disorder according to Our World in Data. Several sources state that 37% of children under 18 years of age have anxiety and the statistics are on the rise.

Today, every state offers a free course on Mental Health First Aid for Adults and Teens and a certificate upon completion. It's a tremendous step in becoming familiar with Mental Health Awareness during crisis. Recently, the American Association for Christian Counselors offered scholarships to church leaders and members who were interested in Mental Health Coaching for the churches and community due to the staggering statistics regarding the increase in opioid overdoses, suicides and mental health crisis.

Back to Texas. One of the group members stated, "Cheryl, maybe your answer is back home in Michigan."

I answered, "Yes, I believe it is." We decided to return to Ypsilanti before Benny was discharged from the halfway house. Eastern Michigan University Family Housing rented me a unit next door to our former apartment.

While packing, I heard familiar footsteps and said, "That sounds like Benny, but it just can't be." It was! They released him from the halfway house a few days earlier without any notification. He destroyed the packed boxes, and took my one thousand dollars while I was asleep. I called the movers and explained the situation. In spite of their rules that all packages must be correctly packed, they agreed to move us from Zephyr Road in Killen, Texas. Thank You Jesus. Abused women, beware. It's imperative that you consult your local Battered Women's shelter for the information, knowledge and correct timing to leave your home and the perpetrator. What works for one, may not be the same plan that works for you. Please seek wise counsel and adhere to the safe plan. Thank you Jesus. The National Domestic Violence Hotline Number is 1-800-799-7233.

I'd began to use that term because by then I was getting religious or more importantly, seeking for a spiritual lifestyle. Shawnie and I attended several churches in Killeen, Texas; Baptist, Jehovah's Witness, Methodist and Muslim just trying to find peace. Things had to get better!

While the movers were in the house, they asked for cash in advance, but Benny still had my money. Drawing a pair of huge scissors I tried to stab him as I screamed, "Give me my money! I'd rather die than live here with you another minute! He knew I meant it, and gave me nine-hundred of the one thousand dollars. We left!

On the train, a book entitled, "Something More", by Catherine Marshall caught my eye. Again I heard that comforting voice say, "Cheryl, I have something more for you." I was still in search of love. Yet, I felt closer to it; that something good was about to happen. I sensed it in the air.

Most of my hair had fallen out. My female system stopped functioning for months. I lost fifteen pounds on my tall, five-feet, nine-and-one-half inch frame. I barely weighed one-hundred pounds. When I smiled, huge knots in my head ran with puss. For the first time I could not mask my pain with a smile. I was a mad black woman, and as long as I remained angry and never moved to the place of the real emotion, hiding under this secondary emotion, I'd never get healed. I would remain angry. Now, I was tired of being angry all of the time.

Anger has four sources: hurt, fear, frustration, and injustice. I had to find the real source and face it.

Several doctors tried to help. But the dermatologist, neurologist, psychiatrist, chiropractor and other physicians stated, "It's your nerves. You are stressed out." My shell was slowly cracking. Their clinical diagnosis was consistent with the psychiatrist in Texas.

Therapy sessions were similar. I remember the therapist's first comment, "You're a strange lady. You don't have the profile that most emotionally disturbed people have. You don't come from a broken home, nor one with alcoholism or drug addiction. You appear very competent and confident. You have a college degree, and are a very gifted teacher. Yet, you don't like yourself."

Confused and angered, I answered, "I know my family loves me, that's what confuses me too. If I didn't love myself, why am I searching for help? I want help, I just don't know how to get rid of this sick feeling. This black cloud rides with me everywhere I go and nothing ever eases it."

I continued receiving counseling and returned to Eastern to pursue a Master's Degree in Sociology. My favorite Sociology Professor became my mentor and was grooming me to be a teaching fellow. I became his graduate assistant but, I transferred to the Counseling Department to prepare to help troubled people such as myself. I learned it takes time and practice, but the only way to stop depression and anxiety was to change my perception and to experience correct thinking. I had to work my way through the feelings and begin to see that they won't hurt me.

My adviser, Dr. Van Riper, was such an inspiration and an excellent, supportive role model for future counselors. When I couldn't drive to my counseling practicums in Wayne, Michigan because of anxiety attacks, he gave me a ride that entire semester. I visited his home often and spent meaningful time with his family. I will never forget his kindness in a crisis. I wanted to be just as kind and compassionate as Dr. Van Riper. My purpose for life and living was becoming clearer, even in the midst of a crisis. I learned how to Listen, an invaluable life skill.

Attending school one hour and sleeping sixteen hours a day became my pattern for months. I loved my counseling classes and consumed self-help books by the hundreds, still looking for life's answers through education. With the exception of my senior year in high school and freshman year in college, I was always an exceptionally good student and sought validation and satisfaction through learning. My pursuits for happiness were endless before I decided to return to Eastern Michigan University to earn my Masters' Degree.

I was the first of twelve African American faculty members hired at one time into a predominantly Caucasian school system. I wanted to improve the students' quality of life and make a difference. Once, during a race riot at the high school, the police were sending all African American students home. When the police officer approached me to send me home, I replied, "Sir, I am not a student, I'm a teacher."

His response was, "I don't care who you, you are Black and you must leave the building, now. Go home." Once again, racism, the reminder that no matter how I tried to improve my quality of life and break the generational curse, I seemed unsuccessful. I internalized an underlying message from a broken lens that day. "We are devalued as a race, and will never be good enough, nor measure up in others eyesight." In retrospect, the police officer was basically protecting me and simply doing his job, however, systemic racism and unrest, the root of an "unloving spirit" was still manifesting itself. How do I change without running? Anxiety caused me to run. There is no need to run, but I kept running because higher education alone wasn't my answer.

I chose education because I loved people and believe that teachers are the shapers and molders of young minds. "I'd graduated to a middle-class profession, but was still forced to live in lower income housing. In Ann Arbor, after reporting my earnings to the Social Services, I still qualified for Aid to Dependent Children.

Still running, I tried to find another interesting occupation to pursue and began attending Transcendental Meditation classes. I even asked my counselor if they had scholarships that would sponsor me to go to Switzerland to sit and meditate in the Swiss Alps for four months, enabling me to be a Transcendental Meditation instructor when I returned. He eyed at me strangely. I knew the answer was No!

Still running, I tried modeling. I graduated from a modeling school in Detroit, only to discover that the director of the school was stabbed to death fifty-two times and his lover left him dead in a motel. I was devastated when they told me he resembled shredded wheat.

Still running, I tried enrolling in a computer school to get me out of the classroom. Two days before I was to begin, I suggested the program to my brother, Butch, a Viet Nam veteran, enrolled and thrived.

Still running, I decided I wanted to be a nurse so I could really help people, but after I fainted from the hospital smells and the patient had to get out of her bed and help me, I changed my mind, but completed the volunteer candy striper program. Next, I decided I wanted to be a court reporter, but there weren't any court reporter schools in the area.

I finally stopped running, made a choice and determined that I was a good teacher and would make an excellent counselor, if I could just discover more about this sickness that kept me feeling sad and distracted.

Being depressed greatly impaired my decision-making processes. Psychological counseling helped me to understand some of the symptoms of the depression, but, did not cure nor eliminate the cause. I was given endless prescriptions for addictive tranquilizers. The doctors also gave me prescriptions for sleeping pills. I had pills to sleep, pills to wake up, pills to function throughout the days, pills to increase my appetite, pills, and pills. I needed something more. One day I looked in my medicine cabinet and yelled, "I'm sick of living like this! Somebody help me!" I threw all of the bottles out. Caution: Don't stop taking any of your medication without your doctor's advice.

Brokenness robs you of your health and God's Original Intent for us, wholeness. It sends you on a wild goose chase and bamboozles you into looking for love in all the wrong places. I tried to get away from my abusive father and married someone who was abusive. The generational pattern of abusive husbands in my family reinforced the self-rejection and rejection that I experienced for years and made it difficult, if not seemingly impossible for me to live without the abuse. That's all I've seen modeled before me as love, and that's all I've learned. At one point during this abuse, I felt like I deserved to be beaten, ignored and neglected because it was comfortable. But, God created us in love, we are wired that way. We are to give love, to be loved, to be secure, to be valued, to feel safe, to have a fulfilling purpose that motivates us to be significant and leave a meaningful legacy and I'm not settling for anything less. My purpose is to learn to celebrate the love God gave me.

The second step in my healing was becoming responsible for finding and facing the brokenness of depression and anxiety and accept my role in participating with my well-being. We recognize we must overcome this romantic relationship stronghold or addiction. Stop trying to fix our unmet childhood relationships with people places and/or things.

As adults we become responsible for making choices that will change and improve the quality and longevity of our lives. However, we must realize until we change our thinking we will continue to unconsciously attract people with the same love deficiencies from their childhoods. We developed and embrace them because they feel comfortable and familiar. Being responsible for healthy boundaries help accomplish the goals toward wholeness.

Boundaries helped me define who I am as an individual. Boundaries sets limits which included my personal likes, dislikes, beliefs and protected me from being manipulated, used, or violated by others. Boundaries helped me to "guard my heart."

God given boundaries, before the foundation of the world, would help me become the original person God created me to be, before I became this imposter hidden in protective patterns.

As I became responsible I began to heal from my character defects and made better choices in alignment with my purpose and destiny. I could change my distorted perception and develop correct thinking. It was never God's original intention that we would suffer from the evil that we've experienced. Before we can be placed in authority we must be positioned under God's authority because God was also establishing boundaries for whole, healthy, secure relationships and protecting us from evil.

My identity would be restored and I would live an abundant life. What I really needed was a fresh start! I really, really wanted to start life over again. I knew I had value and worth in spite of life's experiences. Could I really just start all over again, could I be born a second time? I hope so.

SECTION TWO: WORTH AND VALUE

CHAPTER 3
YOU MUST BE BORN AGAIN

Wanting to start life all over again was my innermost desire. Fix me, make me over again. I despise being a co-dependent, suffering with "the disease of losing myself while depending on others for my unmet needs." Satan used my legitimate need to be loved and accepted in an illegitimate way to produce codependency. While still looking for love in all the wrong places, at Eastern Michigan University, I met a truly saved Christian woman, Sister Pamela Turner, walking down the path from Family Housing, to the main campus.

I asked, "Have any new clubs opened? I've been out of town for a while. What's happening around here now?"

She replied, "I don't have the time nor the desire to go to nightclubs. By the time I attend classes, church and care for my four sons, I just don't have time. There is a joy in knowing Jesus. He is going to save my husband when he comes home from prison. He's in prison serving time for manslaughter. He killed his girlfriends' son with his bare hands. But, Jesus is going to save him. He is also going to save my emotionally ill son and heal my brain damaged boy."

She mentioned other problems as she continued to witness to me. But she had hope and joy. Pamela was indeed a true and living witness of the miraculous works of Jesus Christ. She got my attention. I remember thinking, she has more problems than I do and yet she has a hope. Her husband did all these things, yet she loves him? What kind of love is this? Whatever she has I want it. That's what I've been looking for. She invited me to one Wednesday night Bible Class in Ann Arbor, Michigan. I don't remember a word that was taught, but I went to the altar for prayer. Strange things began to happen after Elder Avery Dumas, Sr. prayed for me.

Shawn, my male friend, escorted me to a club to celebrate my birthday, but I began to lose the desire to wear make-up, dance or anything, saying, "it's not even worth the money I spent to put the make-up on to attend these clubs." A few days later, I found myself visiting another Apostolic Church. While I was there, I made an appointment with the pastor to inquire about changing my life. That meeting was Saturday evening, July 5, 1975, at 8 o'clock in the pastor's living room. I could hardly wait. On Friday, the Fourth of July holiday, I just sat at home all day, eagerly awaiting the appointment.

THE CHRISTIAN SHELL

No more drinking, no more drugs, no more men, no more partying, my friends and relatives thought I was sick! The day and hour finally came when I was ushered into now, the late Elder Jesse Ross's home. Dressed with a very short red and white mini skirt, a navy blue sleeveless shell, a short curly wig and weighing one hundred pounds, at 5'91/2", I looked a sight. He didn't cringe at my outfit, he didn't reject me, but invited me to sit down.

My first question was, "Why is this religious belief different from all other denominations? What makes this one so different?"

He answered, "It's not a religion, nor is it the denomination or church you attend, but it's in obeying Jesus command to be born of the water and of the spirit. The Apostles Doctrine teaches you how to live as Jesus commands. When you are born again, the baptism in Jesus Name is necessary for the remission, removal and forgiveness of your sins. You receive authority in Jesus' Name. The blood is in the name. Then you need the Holy Ghost, God on the inside of you to give you power to change and live holy."

He testified, "When I was an orphan, I felt unloved. I became an alcoholic and wasted my life for years. However, while I was in the U.S. Army, I received the Holy Ghost while stationed in Hawaii." He said further, "The Holy Ghost will lead you to the fullness of the truth about your true worth and value. When I understood my true worth and value because of the cost and price that was paid for me at the cross by Jesus Christ, I was healed of my alcoholism, got married at thirty-nine and was recently elected pastor at sixty-eight years old."

Not understanding too much, I asked, "How do you receive the Holy Ghost?" My feeling was that this might not work for me because I'd tried everything else. Men, education, travel, modeling, transcendental meditation. You name it, I tried it. He asked, "If I give you a gift, what do you have to do to receive it?"

"Take it."

He said, "Well, then, why not?"

"This is what I need. This is it. I'll get baptized tomorrow. "

Elder Ross said, "I'm sure the saints will rejoice with you on tomorrow, but can't you be baptized tonight?"

"Tonight?" I never heard of being baptized as soon as you were ready. Because I was truly ready to change, turn from my sins, wash that guilt away. I cried, "YES! I'm ready! This by far was the greatest decision that I ever made in my entire life, I have repented." Repent, change your mind, change your life, turn into the right direction, stop living the American Dream and now become the dream of God. Repent, repent, repent. I was returning back to the original intention that God had for me and reestablishing Godly boundaries. When we repent we no longer live by the law of sin and death, but we commit to live by the law of life in Christ Jesus which is found in Romans 8:1,2.

My entire life flashed before me. In retrospect I remembered the co-worker at the Ann Arbor Public Schools who used to conduct Bible studies asked me, "Are you saved?"

My response was, "Yes, I was baptized both as a Baptist and a Methodist."

The man gave me a puzzled look, but never said anything else. Not understanding the true meaning then, I told him what salvation meant to me, being baptized and attending church on holidays and Sundays.

I remembered, as children, we'd passed an Apostolic Storefront Church every day as we walked to the corner store on Mc Nichols. We peeked in the door, when we heard the tambourines, and watched the congregation sing and dance. I remember saying," I want to be that happy someday."

The face of that Apostolic, young man who was really witnessing to me and showing me the love of God flashed before me. Mrs. Cranford, our sanctified babysitter, lived on Lumpkin and taught Bible Study to the neighborhood children and gave them milk and cookies. In hindsight, she prayed for us. I thought of Sister Cheryl Bass-Bowles invitations to revivals that I'd turned down. I remembered the invitations to the Bible Studies during lunch taught at Pioneer High School that I turned down. After those memories, I thought of the message, Something More. It all made sense. The Bible verse I recited for grace before dinner daily, "And ye shall be my people and I will be your God" in Jeremiah 30:22, made sense now. These prophetic words of life are a reality. Yes.

We drove a few blocks to a small, white Apostolic Church on a hill called Messias Temple. Sister Cheryl Bass-Bowles and the late Sister Dorothy Bass met us there. Sister Bass said, "Oh, you're, Cheryl Bass, the Lord has had me calling your name in prayer for quite some time, I knew it wasn't my daughter because she's married now." She continued to chat as she dressed me for baptism, "This is the first day of your life. Your battle will always be on your knees in prayer." I had no understanding then, but now I understand. Prayer Is Vital To The Process. "Prayer is one of our greatest weapons."

When Elder Ross baptized me on Saturday, July 5,1975, over 45 years ago, he uttered life changing words. “My dearly beloved sister, upon the confession of your faith which is in the death, burial and resurrection of the Lord Jesus Christ and your confidence in the blessed Word of God; I now indeed baptize you in the Name of The Lord Jesus Christ for the remission of your sins and you shall receive the gift of the Holy Ghost.” Afterwards he lifted me out of the water, and I felt as though a one-hundred pound weight had been lifted off of my shoulders. As the song says, "My burdens rolled away."

Sister Bass helped me to get dressed. She continued sharing about Spiritual Warfare which I didn’t understand at the time. Oh, but what a priceless, life-saving tool prayer is. Sitting on the front pew, the altar workers began to tell me, "Say Hallelujah over and over again. It is the highest praise unto Jesus. He eventually takes control of your tongue and speaks through you in other tongues, in a heavenly language."

Today, altar workers have several methods that each church shares when you desire to receive the gift of the Holy Ghost. I have several friends who received the Holy Ghost before they were baptized, they were ready for a change, repented and they were filled in their homes, on their jobs, in the bathroom, on the airplane. Whenever you get sick and tired of being sick and tired of your mediocre life, repent. It’s not just a onetime mindset. In fact, if we repented daily, there would be a freshness in our lives that exists.

About ten minutes later, strange words come out of my mouth. Talking, and sounding really different, I felt a warm sensation throughout my body. The aches, pains, heartaches, disappointments, depression and anxieties began to leave as I continued to speak in that strange language. The altar workers stopped me and asked, "What happened?" I'd just start speaking over and over again until one hour later a powerful force knocked me back across the pew and the most beautiful song in tongues came out of my mouth. Elder Ross stood up, smiled, and walked toward the door. Those around me began to laugh and ask me, "What happened?"

"I received the Holy Ghost? Are you sure? How do you know you have received the Holy Ghost?" "I heard myself speak in other tongues."

"That's it." They danced and shouted, "Thank You Jesus" and danced with joy as we left the church. It was imperative that I knew that I received the Holy Ghost, because of the test and trials that were waiting for me. I had to know beyond a shadow of a doubt that I was saved according to the Bible. Salvation caused me to shift from living to get my unmet needs met to living for my God and my God given purpose. I now have a new identity, worth and value in Jesus Christ.

I kept running and looking for love and peace in my life until I ran into the loving arms of a Wonderful Savior, The Lord, Jesus Christ. Dr. Charles Stanley, a Christian psychologist and pastor states in St. John 3:3-5,"Jesus answered and said unto him, Verily, verily, I say unto thee; Except a man be born again, he cannot see the kingdom of God...Nicodemus saith unto him, How can a man be born again when he is old? Can he enter the second time into his mother's womb and be born again? Jesus answered, Verily, verily, I say unto thee, except a man be born of the Spirit, he cannot enter into the kingdom of God. Jesus was teaching Nicodemus that physically you can't be born two times in your mothers' womb."

King David explains our human condition in Psalms 51:6 "Behold, I was born shapened in iniquity; and in sin did my other conceive me." We were all born as sinners with the propensity to sin by either self-inflicting wounds or other inflicted wounds as an enemy of God.

Jesus further explains to Nicodemus, a religious ruler who came to him at night, that neither his power, position, prestige, good works, religious beliefs or belief in religious leaders would allow him entrance into Heaven. The Bible says our righteousness is as filthy rags (Isaiah 64:6).

Dr. Stanley continues, "The second birth is a spiritual experience. Salvation is the one time event when God imparts eternal life for those who are dead in their sins. Being born again is an experience that shifts you from living as a human being in a human experience to living as a spiritual being in a human experience. In order to see and to enter the Kingdom of God, living where we acknowledge the Sovereign Rule of God, we must be born again. Being born again is a Spiritual experience where Jesus Christ convicts us of our sins and we surrender to an intimate relationship with Him. We receive; change in relationship; change in position; change in attitude; change in destination.

The second birth is where the Holy Ghost convicts you of your sins and we understand that God loves us in spite of our sins, and good works aren't adequate. Receiving the Holy Ghost shows the evidence of a transformation in our hearts and minds beyond a shadow of a doubt. Nicodemus was a good person like many people, but Jesus said he needed a radical change."

God will speak to our hearts as He spoke to mine and eventually I not only recognized the voice of God, I finally gave Him a proper response. I desperately wanted and needed a change.

When I made the choice by confessing in my heart, turned to Him in repentance, surrendered, obeyed by being baptized of the water and of the spirit, and submitted, God made the radical change on the inside. When we make the choice, God makes the change. I received the gift of the Holy Ghost and what a wonderful gift it is. I realized it's my relationship with God and not my works of righteousness that's important to God. I was no longer an enemy of the cross. I changed in position from being separated from God, to becoming a son of God, in Christ.

No more alcohol, partying, cursing, marijuana, stealing, fighting, depression or blackouts. Each day was worth living. Old things had passed away. All things had changed and become new.

At last I'd realized the love I'd searched for all my life. Jesus was the lover of my soul. He fulfilled all my longings to be loved. Speaking to Jesus through prayer was very fascinating. Through prayer a message came, "Send him out the door." I pondered, "What in the world does this mean?" I recognized His voice, but I failed to respond properly. Jesus was also sending a two-fold warning regarding two boundary breakers that were coming to attempt to dismantle my newfound faith and relationship with Him. Unbeknown to me at that time, I was introduced to spiritual warfare very early. I could recognize the familiar voice of God that protected me all of my life, but was still learning to respond to Him.

Satan immediately attempted to discredit Jesus because my entire motivation for getting saved was to escape my problems and experience more favorable life circumstances. Jesus knew that Benny was coming back into our lives and He knew the pain we'd experience, if we allowed him to intrude again. I failed to discern the warning because I'd only been saved for one month. Two weeks after I was saved, Benny's cousin raped me and I was angry, devastated, afraid and really confused. I was naïve and failed to discern the harmful situation because I was witnessing to his cousin before this crisis and felt that God was protecting me. I no longer felt worthy of God's blessings, but filthy. I blocked it out of my memory for 42 long years, until I was enlarging this newest edition of the book, three years ago.

I want to thank God for the help that He sent me all these years through His church and the brave women of "The Me Too Movement." If they hadn't come forth, I would still be stuck, as a mediocre Christian, still moving two steps forward and three steps backwards. God sent help to walk me through that trauma as I am completing this book. Note: It's important that all traumas are processed through whatever resources are available in the church and/or community i.e. rape counseling, otherwise it stunts anyone's emotional growth and spiritual maturity at the age of the unprocessed trauma. Please just don't stuff it, repress it or pray it away without processing the feelings from the traumatic event and receive healing. Get help, get up, get over it and keep it moving. I didn't say that it was easy, but I'm saying, Psalms 147:3 is a promise where, "He healeth the broken in heart and bindeth up their wounds."

Back to Benny. He had been in a tank accident in Texas, where he'd incurred a fractured face. After receiving a medical discharge, he returned to Michigan and wanted us to remarry. He said, "I thought you said you was saved, you should help me, and I need help! What kind of Christian are you?" Some of the traditional teachers in the church advised me to remarry him, so I decided maybe it was best for me to remarry him. Benny got saved and we remarried. But God never intended for me or anyone to be abused.

My husband was immediately delivered from heroin. No more withdrawals, no pain, cramps, nausea, chills, fevers, shakes, sleepless nights, hustling money or lying. He was no longer a womanizer. He was delivered! Benny enjoyed singing in the church choir, traveling with the church, witnessing about Jesus Christ and His healing power. He even led a song, "Make Me an Example." There really was a radical change in both of us, especially Benny. We had become Soul-Winners and would tell everyone our testimony about how the bad news in your life can become the good news when you are Born Again.

For the first time in seven years, we were a real family. My six year old daughter and I couldn't have been happier that she finally had two parents together. However, Benny hadn't learn that in our flesh, humanity, we still have the Adamic nature or propensity to sin. He believed a false concept concerning deliverance, as many Christians do. He believed that the initial moment he was saved that he no longer had any responsibility to maintain his deliverance. Even though I made new friends within the church, Benny never changed his old associates. He sincerely tried to witness to them by spending time with them in the dope dens. Benny ignorantly believed that, even when he injected heroin, Jesus miraculously would prevent him from getting high.

After salvation, the deep wounds remain in our memories until we grow and transform them through a process of time. Salvation is not a finished work, but a beginning process for us to become who God has called us to be. Some saints like Benny and I got stuck and trapped during the process of sanctification. God knew that we needed extra, tender, loving pastoral care until we could heal and mature into this new lifestyle. God created "community", the church, to become witnesses to the world that sinners can be transformed into saints. He gave us people that we could trust and were capable of walking us through our new process.

Holiness is a way of life. The Christian disciplines of Bible studying, praying, fasting, singing, shouting, praising and worshipping can become ritualistic. When these disciplines are habitual, it's merely works of self-effort adhering to the law of rules and regulation expecting changes without the application, without meaning and purpose. If our lives aren't lived in obedience to God with a pure, sincere, honest heart, then we are subject to be governed and controlled once again by our old man, our former life. Ephesians 5:3 states, "But fornication, and uncleanness, or covetousness, let it not be named among you, as becometh saints." Many Christians were coming to church, but never learned how to come to God through Christ.

Our mature mentors were teaching us how to be accountable as Christian soldiers. God sent the help and it's always a choice whether we will receive it or not. I remember not knowing that certain behaviors were wrong, and I was breaking spiritual boundaries, until Sister Vivian Williams saw me one day, and said, "I remember witnessing to you at the Fletcher Elementary School. I was rejoicing when I saw you a few weeks ago at church when they introduced you as the newest member, because you got saved the night before. I haven't seen you since." I told her I'd been out of town at a party, but, didn't drink and had planned on coming to church occasionally.

She asked me to attend noonday Bible class because I needed to get an understanding of what is required to live a new lifestyle, holiness. When I repented at the altar God restored me. She and others taught me the disciplines of Christ. I was actually like a newborn baby, dependent on others to help me until I grew in grace. God used her to help break the old childhood perception of attending church for an impure motive, satisfying our parents, in order to participate in other activities on Sunday. That's religiosity and not spirituality.

We continued our spiritual journey together for 43 years until God called Vivian D. Williams home on August 6, 2018, to be with Him. She was a true soul winner, comedian and friend. We actually lived like the early church where we continued steadfastly in the Apostles Doctrine and fellowship, and in breaking of bread, and in prayers with other trench buddies and mentors. We also continued together daily with the entire church "with one accord." Messias Temple church members emulated the early church and we experienced unconditional acts of kindness that are acknowledged and shared in other versions that are still available today.

God literally raised up mental health life coaches in their own right during a very challenging time in our marriage. The essence of the roles they fulfilled can be summarized by their Christ like actions to fulfill Jesus Christ mission to the churches stated in St. Luke 4:18-19, "The Spirit of the Lord is upon me, because he hath anointed me to preach the gospel to the poor; he hath sent me to heal the brokenhearted, to preach deliverance to the captives, and recovering of sight to the blind, to set at liberty them that are bruised, To preach the acceptable year of the Lord." Jesus said that He came to heal the broken hearted so they could be completely set free. Jesus mission was to minister unconditional love, the only way that broken hearted people will be restored and healed. Broken-hearted people have one thing in common; they feel unloved, unworthy and inadequate, even after being born again, until they begin to grow in the grace, discover their worth and value in God and learn how to celebrate the love that God gave.

When God revealed that Shawnie was paying a price during this unhealthy marriage, I finally set new boundaries. I took control of my life and said, "No!" I learned how to overcome the anxiety that I felt in my body and the guilt. I was overcoming the fear of losing Benny when I recognized this is not pleasing God. I'd been afraid of confrontation and truly believed I was maintaining peace and doing things God's way, but that was a broken generational pattern.

This day was different. I knew I'd given this marriage to God and trusted Him for my life. I was more valuable to God and was living beneath my God-given privilege by cowering down to please Benny rather than pleasing God. God wasn't pleased that I was the recipient of sinful, abusive behavior. I was finally setting limits on abuse. As a child, I never felt safe enough to say No, but I was learning to make healthy choices as God re-parented me.

"No" to a perpetrating, abuser is like a curse word and an act of defiance. To my horror, I watched as he took an axe and swung it backwards and forwards and hacked our glass tables, as I heard them shatter. I told Shawnie to run to our neighbors for help as I ducked to keep from getting hit. He threw my twenty-eight plants, one by one, against the living room wall. He destroyed everything in our home.

"Oh, my Lord, I yelled, Jesus, Jesus, Help Us." He stopped and left the house. It took my daughter and me several days to clean the mud and dirt off the yellow walls and carpet.

Something came alive in me that day. I was grateful to God for sparring our lives. I was finally learning that God really is my "safe place." He will never leave you nor forsake you**.** My spirit received the end of the matter, a resolve, concerning this marriage. I received a spiritual release before it was finally over. The false belief, or toxic faith, that I held onto for years, was broken, and the truth regarding our marriage was eventually revealed. It's important that young people and adults discern the truth.

Just because children pray that their parents will remain married, and they don't or mates pray that their mates will change and they don't, doesn't mean that God doesn't love us; nor that we failed because we didn't have enough faith. Just because we pray that our loved ones will be healed and they die doesn't mean that we missed God's voice or His mindset. It meant that God is Sovereign and knows all of our hearts and how much we can bear. The prayers we prayed didn't change the situation, but it changed us on the inside to accept the adversity, to grow and mature from it. We learn to understand that we won't always understand, but God is Sovereign and He knows. I died out to my will and slowly accepted God's will and stopped fighting to retain control and attempting to make our marriage work. Marriage requires two partners who are willing participants in improving the quality and longevity of one another's lives.

When I knew that I was free to leave this abusive marriage, I packed my car to leave because enough is enough. But my friends unpacked it, because we were taught we needed to obey the marriage vows. "Wait on Jesus." I probably reluctantly consented to maintain an image.

I believe today many "church hurts" are caused by many well-meaning Christians who adhered to the rituals, traditions, rules and regulations of the church rather than living by the Spirit of God. I myself, failed to discern the move of the Spirit that day based on my intimate relationship with God. He was actually releasing me from the abusive marriage, that day. However, once again, I recognized God's voice but failed to respond correctly and depended on the opinions of others. My feeling of value was at the mercy of what others thought about me. My sense of identity was determined by how others responded to me. Yet, God was teaching me that I was Holy-Ghost filled, but needed to learn how to be Holy-Ghost led. Proverbs 29:25, "Fear of man will prove to be a snare, but whoever trusts in the Lord is kept safe." I paid a costly price and consequences for my missed opportunity and day of deliverance.

I finally asked, "Well Lord, what is your will concerning Benny? I know according to your Word that it is your will that all men be saved."

"He answered by showing me a vision of Benny's funeral, a scripture in Ezekiel 3:19 which states, "If thou warn the wicked, and he turn not from his wickedness, nor from his wicked way, he shall die in his iniquity; but thou hast delivered thy soul." When I shared what God revealed to me, they said, Oh Sister Bass, you hate Benny so that you wish he was dead." No, I love my husband, I'm just sharing with you what God shared with me. Once again, now, spiritual parents sharing that I was mistaken and that Benny wasn't going to die, triggered the old doubt in my heart. However, I thanked God for a confirmation that came from one of the young elders prophesying an early death if Benny did not repent of his sins and return to serve him. The Lord pronounced judgment on Benny, if he didn't repent. Please note how important repentance is.

One day, feeling troubled in my spirit, I realized that Benny was in danger. He'd been missing for three days. Finally, when he returned home, he staggered and I knew he was ill. It wasn't unusual for him to have infections from the needle he used during drug abuse, however, this time God revealed something was different.

While preparing to attend our church council that Saturday in December, late 1970's, the Lord said, "Stay home, anoint Benny's right arm and take him to the hospital. In obedience, we took him to

Veteran's Hospital in Ann Arbor, Michigan. The doctor yelled immediately, "We are going to amputate his right arm."

I contacted Elder Ross, told him what the doctor said, and he dropped the phone. Sister Ross picked up the phone and said, "Papa is on his knees praying right now." Within minutes, the second doctor stated, "We can save his arm, admit him for four days, treat the infection and discharge him."

The next day at the Sunday morning service, I testified how Jesus heard Elder Ross's prayer and within minutes miraculously changed the doctor's decision to amputate, and spared his arm. When Jesus sends a promise it is important to believe Him no matter what happens. No matter what.

At the hospital, I waited in Benny's empty room on the fourth floor for a long time. I knew nothing except he was out of his room for tests. Being led to the third floor by the Lord, I called my parents from the pay phone, even though there were phones on the fourth floor. I observed the doctors rushing my husband quickly down the hall. Yelling and stopping one of the doctors, he turned and said, "There's his wife." He told me, "We are going to amputate his right arm, shoulder and back."

Shocked, I screamed, "Oh, Lord! No!" I remember the promise, we can save his arm, admit him for four days, treat the infection and discharge him.

The doctor continued, "We are trying to save his life, he has gas gangrene which is spreading rapidly throughout his body and we only give him a 10/90 chance to live through the night. We're trying to spare his life, lady."

Crying, I stumbled weakly into a phone booth and proceeded to call everyone who could pray. Someone was able to give the message to Elder Ross and he stopped the entire concert where Messias Choir was singing. They told me he led a powerful prayer. In the meantime, Elders Ralph Johnson and Larry Clifton from our church prayed before they came to the hospital and Larry stated the Lord said, "He shall recover." Shawnie told me afterwards that she was with the children at the concert and they kept telling her, that her father was going to die.

Sister Dorothy Bass, was the first saint to arrive at the scene and we watched Benny's heart stop twice on the table and every time we'd say Jesus, it began to beat again. Others arrived shortly around 4 o'clock and my sister, Denise, drove from Detroit, to be supportive.

At 10 o'clock the doctor walked in with a stunned look on his face and said, "He is stronger than we thought, we didn't believe he could live through the night, but he has a 50/50 chance to survive. The gas gangrene is very tricky and he could still die within the next thirty days if it spreads through his system."

Sister Carol Hollis, Elders Ralph Johnson and Larry Clifton, Sister Dorothy Bass, my sister, Denise and myself praised the Lord in that waiting room, with tears of joy flooding our faces. Shortly afterwards, a nurse entered the room. Her face told me the message even before she spoke to me. "The reason the doctors did not amputate is because they did not believe your husband would live through the night. They simply stopped in the middle of the surgery!" We knew it was Jesus who healed him in the midst of the operation.

That night, I laid on my face in the middle of the living room and cried before the Lord in prayer, "Jesus, I know Benny is not worthy to live, but neither am I. Yet I am serving you all I know how. I thought because of the severe abuse that I didn't care whether he lived or died, but don't take him from us. You spared his life tonight, but the doctors are saying he could still die. If I have to stay up all night long in spiritual warfare, interceding and praying, I will."

The Lord simply replied, "Get up, go to bed, you need your rest, I have healed him." In other words, start taking care of yourself, get your own life back, I got this. I'd just been an eye witness to God performing a miracle. I will never forget this miracle all the days of my life.

Many felt that this incident changed him and he'd return to church and be a better husband and father. During his stay in the hospital for thirty days, they opted not to give him drug therapy because they were sure that every time he looked at his arm and had full use of it, even though they did remove his muscle, that he would never abuse drugs again. He was a walking miracle. His arm was supposed to hang without his muscle, but he had full use of his arm. Glory to God.

The very day he was discharged he shot up, and refused the will of the Lord in his life for salvation. I knew he had botched up his last chance. I grieved.

In the midst of this crisis I sought for help. My pastor said he was unable to help us with the great problems we experienced. One of the sisters told me to call District Elder Norman Wagner, now the late honorable Bishop Norman Wagner, in Youngstown, Ohio is known as the man of God. He has a reputation for having several gifts and being able to receive a specific revelatory word from The Lord for my specific situation rather than a ritualistic, random, traditional quote from the scriptures that often created more guilt and frustration.

I was able to correspond with District Elder Wagner for several years before I ever saw him. His letters were very warm and encouraging. I finally met him one Sunday morning after Benny, drove Shawnie and I to Youngstown.

District Elder Wagner was extremely wise and preached It Is The Object of His Will That You Be Happy", once we know God's purpose for our life we have great value and worth like Queen Esther, who came to the kingdom for such a time as this. I was properly discerning that there is a purpose in my pain and suffering.

The crisis with Benny continued, but I had become more hopeful even though I was a codependent, a family member of the drug addict. My pastor prayed and encouraged me continually. He stated his own inability to deal with the new generation's problems of drug addiction.

"Just pray about it," he'd say. "Pray about it."

I repeated, "Pray about it! I'm praying all I know how, and Benny seems to be getting worse."

Elder Ross smiled and said, "I know you don't understand now, but Jesus has a bright future for you in spite of all you're suffering. You will learn that suffering is designed to bring you forth as pure gold." I was "called to suffer in the furnace of affliction" for ministry. God used Benny to teach me how to pray and develop a vertical intimate relationship with Him and eventually surrender completely. I kept on praying and I enrolled in a First Aid Drug Overdose course to understand the effects of the drug. During that time they didn't have a Christian Counselor, nor drug counseling for the families such as Al anon.

Today Alan Botton redefines addiction "as any pattern of behavior whereby you can't stand to be with yourself and with your uncomfortable thoughts and emotions that come from being with yourself or on your own." He continues to teach "you can be addicted to anything as long as it keeps you away from yourself, self-knowledge.... This addiction guarantees that you remain distracted and lack self-knowledge. Until you know yourself, you cannot have a healthy relationship." Therefore, an addiction is whatever you set your affections on that is greater than a true relationship with God, whether it's a substance or distractions that keeps you running from the truth about yourself.

Whatever our passion is for distractions to intimacy becomes our addiction i.e. marriages where the husbands spend so much time golfing, fishing, hunting, or involved in sports until he neglects his family. Parents may be driven to make money at the expense of their relationships with their children because of a fear of intimacy. Ministers who are so busy attending to the needs of others, sometimes unconsciously neglecting their own families.

Unbeknown to me, I was addicted in my attempts to "rescue" Benny. God doesn't want rescuing, do-good Christians. He wants Godly Christians who are kind and who are led by the spirit to do good works, not driven by good works. Many of God's people are spirit-filled but not spirit-led. Spiritual, emotional and physical burnout is real in leadership. I experienced "burnout for years until God revealed to me, how to live and move in the Spirit. I'm still learning."

I attended The Family Counseling Center at the local community agency and the counselor spent two years counseling me about the guilt and responsibility I felt concerning Benny's drug addiction. He helped me to realize that it was not my responsibility nor my fault, but as a codependent, I was an enabler. "The choice to use drugs is his," the counselor said, but it is not your responsibility to cater to his needs, cover up for him on his job, nor support his drug habit. The sooner you allow him to take consequences for his own actions, the sooner he will hit rock-bottom and begin to confront his illness and seek help."

After that, I refused to make any more excuses for him to the family, friends, church or employers. Setting boundaries is a key principle. I detached and let him live his own life, so I could live mine. I want to live the abundant life. I no longer tried to deny or hide his drug addiction. I was no longer humiliated and embarrassed to tell new friends, colleagues and co-workers that my husband was a heroin addict. So I shifted from feeling ashamed, embarrassed and humiliated to feeling disappointed. I was learning how to check in with my feelings

When I'm feeling trapped, helpless or less than, or irritable and start trying to control something or someone to relieve anxiety, I stop and rehearse The Serenity Prayer: God grant me the serenity to accept the things I cannot change; courage to change the things I can; and the wisdom to know the difference…."

Today, I see some church members as Codependent where we exchange our dependencies on external forces rather than depending on the spiritual development and spiritual discernment from the Holy

Spirit on the inside of us. Spiritual discernment is perhaps one of the most under taught principles that is so important to the success of our spiritual journey.

True spirituality is possessing the Holy Spirit and developing an intimate relationship with God and producing the spiritual fruit of the spirit which sums up nine attributes of Christian living in accordance with the Holy Spirit which develops character. According to Galatians 5:22,23, "But the fruit of the Spirit is love, joy, peace, longsuffering, kindness, gentleness, goodness, faith, meekness, temperance against such there is no law." It's the character of God being developed in our personality that is needed to revive our churches today. There is a shift from focusing solely on developing the spiritual gifts as a sign of spiritual maturity to prioritizing the fruit of the spirit to overcome our character defects, heal damaged emotion, make our crooked, irrational thinking straight and our inappropriate behaviors Christ like.

In addition to the fruit of the spirit, I was to model the privilege we have inherited when we are born again, to allow the Holy Spirit to re-parent us and heal us everywhere that we hurt. The unhealthy perceptions that we developed regarding our father-figures needed to be reframed before we can learn to trust Our Father which art in Heaven. I was learning that knowledge is power, and I was receiving a first-hand education in wisdom how to help hurting people, unbeknown to me at the time.

After salvation the process of sanctification becomes a lifestyle one day at a time. According to Hebrews 6:1, "Therefore leaving the principles of the doctrine of Christ, let us go on to perfection, not laying again the foundation of repentance from dead works and of faith toward God.

I had to repent from doing things my way. Lasting change occurs when we repent. Repentance will produce a change that is progressive. Once we turn to God to meet those unmet needs and completely trust Him, we will be restored.

A person who has been in a wounded state may be blinded to their sinful responses such as anger and bitterness, or the structures of codependency that have developed out of that anger. We must realize that our ways of thinking and acting which developed out of wounding, will not last. Because we have been blinded by our wounds and brokenness, we were blinded to our sinful actions and attitudes. This blindness will keep us in darkness, and give Satan access to continue tormenting us. Genuine repentance is not simply a "rethinking." Repentance must first be rooted in a high value on God, not a high value on oneself. When we repent it leads to the forgiveness of sin, the removal of divine discipline, and the restoration of one's experiential communion with God. A change of mind or perspective is of no value if it isn't accompanied by a change of attitude, a change of direction, a change of life and action.

True repentance is falling prostrate in prayer before God on my face and travailing in prayer and acknowledging that what I did was wrong. I have sinned and God is grieved. Psalms 51:17, paraphrased, "The sacrifices of God are of one's relationship to sin and God, broken spirit and a contrite heart, O God, thou wilt not despise." David acknowledged his sin; he refused to cover his iniquity and he was determined to confess his transgressions. David comes totally clean. He makes no excuses, offers no rationalizations, and refuses to shift blame. Repentance is painful, but it is a sweet pain. It demands brokenness of heart, but always with a view to healing and restoration and a renewed vision of holiness.

The only thing that mattered was living a life that celebrates the love God has given me. I started celebrating the love that GOD has given me by internalizing Psalms 118:24, "This is the day which the Lord hath made, we will rejoice and be glad in it." I wrote Broken to be Made Whole, From Pain to Power and other books as I matured in the process of growing in grace in God.

However, during this long journey I neglected to apply the principles to myself because I didn't take the necessary quiet time and solitude to change. God kept sending warnings and summons me to find the shattered pieces of my heart, give, surrender and release them to God. Now decades later, I was ready to participate with God in my healing and wholeness by given Him the pieces of my broken heart to be restored and stop doing it my way.

The third step was to repent, which means change your mind or to change your focus from your circumstances to God; or change your directions from worldly living and turn towards a spiritual lifestyle. The meaning of repentance is four-fold: change your mind, your behavior, your attitude and your destination. With unmet childhood needs this four-fold repentance requires both a turning from sinful behaviors and the lies we believed when certain needs weren't met, and turning completely to God to meet those needs. Repent for placing man's opinion of who you are over what God says about you. We put too much importance on what people think. Repentance removes the guilt and cleanses wounds the heart and restores our worth and value. Restoration is finally come!

CHAPTER 4
BE RESTORED, LET GOD PUT THE PIECES OF YOUR HEART BACK TOGETHER AGAIN

At one time in my life, I thought I was sitting on top of the world in spite of all the painful experiences of childhood, a bad marriage, poor relationships and even experiencing great struggles after being born-again. In spite of all those adversities, the Lord blessed me and I was able to receive my Master's Degree in Guidance and Counseling in April 16, 1977. Yet, I was still challenged physically, emotionally/mentally and spiritually.

> Feeling like Humpty Dumpty, I compared myself to the egg who fell off of the wall!
> Humpty Dumpty sat on the wall.
> Humpty Dumpty had a great fall.
> All the kings' horses and all the kings' men,
> Couldn't put Humpty together again.

Whoever heard of putting a shattered, broken, scrambled egg back together again, shell and all? What is impossible with all the kings' horses and all the kings' men, is possible with The King of Kings and the Lord of Lords. He specializes in restoring, bringing you back to the original state,

I felt like Humpty Dumpty who fell off of the wall. I felt like I was still searching for the missing pieces of my heart and trying to put them together again myself. Big mistake! Humpty Dumpty, an egg, was symbolic of a fragile person. The egg, however, fragile, holds the potential for the complete life cycle in creation. Humpty Dumpty, with all of life's potential of wholeness embodied in him/her, was sitting on a wall or a fence, just enjoying the view from an elevated position, with false masks of pride, self-importance and facades. So here sits an egg, representing infinite possibilities, not making a choice to live its destiny, afraid to commit to a path of action or to find his/her true purpose on this earth, then live it. He/she was sitting on the wall of indecision, giving into fear. Therefore, he/she fell off the wall of indecisiveness and pretense into the depths of humanity that allowed him/her to penetrate and experience the darkest places of his/her being. The only way to grow is to refuse to allow myself, or Satan or any perpetrator to continue to victimize me again and entrap me in sin by the way I reacted to their behaviors toward me. To continue to seethe in anger, rehearse vengeful thoughts, suppress and repress my emotions and refuse to forgive because of pride and self-sufficiency is sinful. Proverbs 14: 12 states, "There is a way that seemeth right unto a man, but the end thereof are the ways of death."

But I finally realized that even though I never considered myself a person filled with pride, I was like Humpty Dumpty who had a Big Head. My head was filled with negative thoughts of humanism that I learned from the university. Psychology and sociology theories required logical conclusions. All of these thoughts challenged the faith that I needed for my sanctification process in holiness. When I refused to let go of my old beliefs, feelings, and lies, it became too much for my mind and body to handle any more pain. I listened to lies and believed my feelings. I was living an emotional lifestyle. My body rebelled and shut down. I fell off the wall and broke.

One night I was in the bathroom getting ready for church when Benny began to beat and pound on the door, yelling, "Come out of there! I need to use the bathroom!" He used the bathroom daily to "shoot up" his heroin.

"I came out of the bathroom and made a decision not to allow my anger to punch Benny in his face. Instead, I left the house and went to church early. When I was overwhelmed, I made a new choice to surrender to God and not take matters into my own hands. Psalms 61:1,2 states, "From the end of the earth will I cry unto thee, when my heart is overwhelmed: lead me to the rock that is higher than I."

I made the right decision to go to the church for help. After the service, a strange sensation overwhelmed me as I was leaving the restroom, I began to holler, scream, yell and roll all over the restroom floor. Eventually I blacked out. My friends shook me, slapped me, and splashed cold water on my face. They told me it took thirty minutes before Evangelist Yvonne Hawkins, now, Pastor Yvonne Hawkins-

Bell, was able to slap me and bring me back to a conscious state. Resting at my friend, Jewell's home, Jesus spoke to me and said, "Wait, just a little while longer." While we were in prayer, He made promises to us about blessings. He was going to give me a good companion, an anointed ministry, financial prosperity and bless my daughter.

Five months after the anxiety attack, or whatever that experience was in the restroom at church, my health was deteriorating. After another doctor's visit, when my vital signs continued to be very low and dangerous, my physician admitted me to St. Joseph's Hospital in Ann Arbor for nervous exhaustion and malnutrition.

While I was hospitalized for ten days during Thanksgiving (November 21-December 1, 1980). The psychiatrist stated my diagnosis was an ambulatory breakdown due to anxiety neurosis, chronic clinical depression, malnutrition and domestic abuse. They were also concerned about a possibility of severe brain damage. An ambulatory breakdown is a nervous breakdown that required short term hospital care and outpatient treatment at home.

The breakdown was my breakthrough in disguise. The same familiar, sweet voice of the Lord that I experienced before I was saved sent me a message. He said, "Gross darkness will enter your life. At the end of the year, I will deliver you, and lift you up in a high place in me." The sin of unbelief and unforgiveness was unmasked and shattered while the thoughts that caused the feelings were being exposed. At this point in my life, God knew that I needed more than prayer in these deep wounds, but it was the prayers and forgiveness that opened the doors for the help I received.

Before my discharge, the psychiatrist recommended that Shawnie and I go to live in a Battered Persons Shelter. I responded, "No, I cannot live in a Battered Persons Shelter, the Lord is getting ready to deliver me from this crisis."

My church family said, No, give her to us, we'll help her and Jesus will heal her. The church exists not for ourselves, but to get our friends and members in front of Jesus.

The hospital staff just looked at me like they thought I was crazy. One person accused me of being a glutton for punishment. But once again, I heard that sweet voice that I now know was God. He was in every circumstance, setback, obstacle, loss, hurdle, disappointment, sickness, relationship and financial reversal, etc., and He's in this crisis with me right now. If you have continued to read this far, may I take the time to tell you that God is with you right now. There's no wind that's so strong that never stops blowing, and there no road that's so long that it never ends. I can feel you, you're at the end of your rope; but tie a knot at the end of the rope and hang on. Help is on the way. Help is here.

MENTAL HEALTH AND THE CHURCH

Messias Temple modeled successful ministry for Mental Health and The Church. Ypsilanti State Hospital was a mental health hospital on the outskirts of Ypsilanti. It wasn't uncommon to see people living with mental health issues walking within our community. While I was working on my counseling internship, Elder Ross allowed me to host a weekly support group for that Mental Health Agency at the church. My friends assisted me as we showed them love, acceptance and hope. I was healing from my wounds and helping others in the same condition that I was being healed from. II Corinthians 1:4 states, "Who comforteth us in all our tribulation, that we may be able to comfort them which are in any trouble, by the comfort wherewith we ourselves are comforted of God."

Messias Temple was the leading institution in the community that fostered the healing because of "unconditional love." The other community agencies were support systems networking towards our families' wholeness. The Salvation Army Worker was concerned about our finances and the dietitian about my nutritional intake. Benny had restricted visitation rights because he came in my room cursing at me and demanding money.

Upon discharge, my friend, the late Jewell Stallworth-Finley wheeled me out of the hospital. Unable to walk, talk, think, eat, sleep nor drive then, I found I had no shell left. It was shattered everywhere I literally stayed in the bedroom day and night, unable to walk without help. The only time I left the bedroom was when I went to the bathroom, just a few feet away. That short distance seemed like an hour's journey. When I was able to sit up, Shawnie would help me down-stairs and I would sit on the sofa reading the Bible and praying for eight hours a day. When I needed to use the bathroom, I'd crawl upstairs, and slid down the steps. Just like a baby crawls. While sitting on the red sofa, ideas invaded my mind, but reading the Bible would combat those fantasies and racing thoughts that I had to deal with. I was no longer on the wall of indecision, I was no longer trying to retrieve the pieces of my old life, I let go of the old man, and embraced the new man. I was now developing into a true authentic, spiritual leader. God Himself humbled me.

Eating was one of the most difficult tasks. My friend, Evangelist Ivy Caddell, would patiently spoon feed me daily like a baby for months. My stomach was tied up in knots and the food agitated it because I couldn't digest it. Ivy demonstrated unconditional love. She never judged nor belittled me. She taught me if I wanted to get well, that I needed to eat. When I finally learned how to eat more, I could think better. When I could eat and think better, I was able to regain my strength and walk better.

Unbeknown to me at that time, Ivy was hired and trained forty-nine years ago, as a psychiatric nurse's aide at Potlow State Hospital, a state mental institution, in Tuscaloosa, Alabama.

She was employed at the very hospital that doctors wanted to admit her to after she sustained brain injuries from a brick thrown at her head that knocked her ear off during the civil rights unrest. At seventeen years old, her head was swollen, her face was twisted, she was bedridden and only weighed seventy pounds. A holiness evangelist was passing through Tuscaloosa and heard about Ivy's condition. When she came to Ivy's home, she poured an entire bottle of anointing oil on Ivy, prayed for her and told her she would was healed.

Ivy's face straightened immediately, but her family had to spoon feed her. It took five years before she was completely healed and saved. She was hired and trained by psychiatrists and psychologists in a 21 Day Program entitled, Breaking Bad Habits. After her training within two or three months she saw patients improve their quality of life. Some people who crawled to the dining room, now walked into the dining room and sat at the table. Some people who ate like animals with their hands, now ate properly at the dining table. Others who couldn't keep their clothes on, but ran around nude, learned how to dress themselves as well as keep their clothes on.

Isn't that just like Jesus, to prepare Ivy to minister to me after she had been comforted, with the same comfort? I had very little strength to walk and one day after falling in the kitchen, Benny stood over me, laughed at me, and left me lying on the floor. While lying on the floor, I began to pray and knew Jesus was going to deliver my daughter and me. I did have a hope and now a promise, "He healeth the broken in heart and bindeth up their wounds." I wasn't completely broken, but being restored by love.

Jesus immediately answered my prayers. The door happened to be open even though it was winter, and my friend, Sister Nancy Smith, now Min. Nancy McFarland, came to the door, entered the home, helped me up and rebuked Benny. He continued to laugh. After he left, Nancy and I turned to the Lord in one of the most fervent prayers ever prayed. Laying prostate before Him on our faces, we prayed for deliverance. The late Evangelist Eva Siscoe counseled me for years as a separated single sister and used to always say, "The Lord will either draw them to salvation or drive them out of your life." Breakthrough.

Approximately two weeks later on January 11, 1981, Benny left, never to return again. On that very same day Sister Keena Frost helped Shawnie receive the Holy Ghost. My daughter had been seeking it for the six years since her baptism. She was immediately delivered from her migraine headaches. She felt guilty and responsible for our problems. She told me, "I feel half good because of you, and half bad because of Daddy." "Acts 1:8 "and ye shall receive power after the Holy Ghost is come upon you." Breakthrough

After I realized that the Lord would hear and answer my prayers even though I had a breakdown, I learned to love prayer and prayed morning, noon and night. The Bible states that He is nigh to the broken and contrite. I became fascinated knowing that I could kneel down and talk to the Lord and He would bend His ear to hear me. He walked with me and he talked with me. I developed a hunger and thirst after righteousness. Breakthrough

Jesus proceeded to make me over again piece by piece. He began to dismantle the cycle of battering/ abuse and the cycle of rejection. It took years to be healed. I didn't receive an instant miracle. I wanted an instant miracle, but years later while still healing, Bishop Wagner told me after I moved, that Jesus would heal me like the lepers who were healed as they went (process). He healed ten lepers and only one accessed the promise of wholeness because he went back and thanked Jesus for his healing. He was obedient to the directives when Jesus told them to show themselves to the priest. He received more than the others, he was put back together again better than he was before he was afflicted. Likewise, why settle for healing when you can be made whole? Praise and Thanksgiving is now one of my major keys to wholeness. I developed an attitude of gratitude.

Paul addresses the holistic method of living in I Thessalonians 5:23, "And the very God of peace sanctify you wholly; and I pray God your whole spirit, and soul and body be preserved blameless unto the coming of our Lord Jesus Christ." When one of the areas of the trichotomy of man is out of sync, the equilibrium in the spirit-body-mind connection manifests stress related illnesses. Being restored (put back together again), involved total commitment and dedication to change. It requires more energy and discipline to change, than to remain stuck in a painful lifestyle, but it is more beneficial.

District Elder Wagner stated, "The key to change is to realize that in the trichotomy of the spirit, soul and body, the spirit is the real you. But the spirit is often held captive by the soul and body, depending upon the decision the soul makes. The soul is the mind, emotions and intellect (will). If messages are interpreted by the soul without the spirit's input then the person is emotional. The decision and reactions are based solely on feelings and emotions which are unreliable and carnal. Perceptions are in the soul. The spirit is the part that gets its message from God, transmits it to the soul, and the soul interprets the message spiritually and dictates to the body how to behave like Christ.

The Strengthened Shell

The Lord used several compassionate people to help put the pieces of my life back in place again. Church "community" servants and community agency workers networked together, with each one contributing pieces of the shell. The Vocational Rehabilitation counselor wrote my treatment plan and she networked with various agencies after evaluating our unmet needs. The treatment plan included counseling, physical fitness, nutrition, medical care, education and financial support for gas, clothing, automobile repairs, tuition, books, emergencies, and relocation. The bi-weekly meeting with them provided encouragement and the skills to define and achieve short and long term goals.

My new counselor was blind. Her blindness had a great impact on my life because she had focused vision and discernment. She was married, had two children and very dedicated to her career of helping rehabilitate people. The goal of the two year treatment plan was for me to reenter the work force with skills that maximized my strengths and minimized my weakness. It was decided that I should change from a teaching profession to a counseling and social worker profession. Proverbs 29:18, "Without a vision (purpose) my people will perish." Breakthrough

Dr. Deloisteen Brown, our Christian, family physician, provided weekly checkups and encouragement. She explained, "You will be like a baby. You will have to learn how to walk, talk, think, eat, speak and drive all over again. You will have to relearn basic daily living skills. You will also need to consider working as a librarian where the atmosphere is quiet and there is no noise.

"Teaching is too challenging for your temperament. You are blessed that you know the Lord, have a strong family, beautiful daughter, supportive church and an education. Most Black women in your position never prepared themselves to support the family, but you have more assets than you know. This is just a temporary setback. You will need to recuperate for five years, but after that you will be just fine. You are a winner! Romans 8:35–37, "Who shall separate us from the love of Christ? Shall tribulation, or distress, or persecution, or famine, or nakedness, or peril, or sword? Nay, in all these things we are more than conquerors through him that loved us."

We still communicate at least once a year for these forty years. I will never forget her unconditional love, Christ-like gentleness and kindness.

The Black male psychologist provided bi-weekly counseling. During the sessions, forgiveness, self-love, unconditional love and discipline were taught. The synopsis of several counseling sessions are para-phrased:

"You are a strange contradiction. You have great assets. You have not exercised your psychological muscles. You have given the responsibility and control over to others. Whenever you relinquish your control to others they manipulate, use and abuse you.

No one else knows what is best for you except you and the Lord. Learn to command respect, do not expect everyone to like you, but to respect you. Learn to enjoy being with yourself. Spend your quiet time learning how to love yourself. Others will love you, the more you love yourself. Learn to love others without expecting them to give you love in return. If you give love and expect something in return, then you are a taker.

Love yourself by making healthy decisions and wise choices concerning yourself. Although it may feel awkward, and even selfish at first. You have been brainwashed to believe that you are selfish and self-centered, but to the contrary you have catered to everyone else's needs, neglecting your own. You're trying to please people, and now you are angry. You've developed a facade and veneer of self-confidence, smiling and being nice. You smile whenever you are in pain. But people are irritated by nice people, if they are phony. You appear so fragile. They feel guilty, honestly interacting with you. They are unsure of your feelings because you are often unsure of your own feelings. You are a very indecisive person.

Take control of your life, take control of your time, take control of your finances, and resources. Listen to your body and your mind. Self-talk is very important and body talk is significant. Your body will talk to you. If something is not right for you, your gut will talk to you. Don't think with your heart, emotions and feelings, that's what has caused all of your problems. Don't make any decisions when you are hungry, angry, depressed, lonely, tired or in a hurry. When you feel calm and your body is comfortable, then it is the right time for you to make a decision.

Learn to say no and be assertive. People have no problem telling you no. You have to live with their decision in spite of your anger. Let them do the same thing with you. It's not failing your Christian duty to say no. Evaluate your relationships. Many have been controlling, immature, unemotional men, where you have desired to meet unfulfilled childhood needs.

As an adult you are responsible for your own happiness. Your parents are not accountable for your well-being. You must forgive any injustices you feel occurred while growing up. Loving yourself means making an inventory of your strengths and weaknesses and being aware of both. Always seek to maximize strengths and minimize weaknesses.

Don't place yourself in situations that cause anxiety. Always have a realistic expectation of yourself. Your daughter will need counseling by another female role model because she has been modeling you during your depression as you modeled your mother. You can help her as you change. She will change. The best thing you can ever do for your daughter is to change.

You will also need the support of a group to give you more feedback for daily living skills than the two hours a week we meet. It will expedite your healing. Clinical, chronic depression usually requires two years of therapy. You will also be awarded a scholarship to attend the weekend group therapy retreats because of your financial situation. You will also need a relative or friend to accompany you because the pain will be overwhelming and anxiety provoking at times."

My sister and brother-in-law, at that time, were my supports and this fostered healing. Denise, once again, shared how much she loved me and how I was her role model. She stated, "I don't know why you think you are so passive. I'm the one who was passive compared to you. You have boldness, you have become someone else, but the real you is assertive." I felt revived when she expressed her love. Breakthrough

The psychologist continued to provide a holistic treatment plan as he stated, "Follow this eighteen day fast menu to eliminate the toxins and poisons from your body. Two days you will eat salads, poultry, brown grains, and baked potato for lunch and dinner, light fruit and grain for breakfast. Three days you will consume nothing but liquids. Pure fruit juices, distilled water and lemon water. Continue this process for eighteen days. You will experience a weight loss, but you will feel much better.

Your anger and un-forgiveness has affected your emotional state, and you have turned them inward. Learn to use anger constructively. When you are angry with someone else it is often because you see yourself in that person and that annoys you. That's why children who mirror their parents often clash because people hate to see themselves. Another reason for anger is that someone refuses to allow you to control them."

The psychologist was a great support. The counseling sessions were painful and draining at times. The long fast was a very healthy experience. My thinking became extremely clear while I simultaneously read the New Testament in fifty days. That became a revival, renewal and a refreshing time. Ephesians 4:22- 32, "That ye put off concerning the former conversation the old man, which is corrupt according to deceitful lusts; And be renewed in the spirit of your mind; And that ye put on the new man, which is after God is created in righteousness and true holiness....Be ye angry, and sin not: .....neither give place to the devil.....let no corrupt communication proceed out of your mouth, but that which is good to the use of edifying, that it may minister grace unto the hearers.....be ye kind one to another, tenderhearted, forgiving one another, even as God for Christ's sake hath forgiven you." Breakthrough

The group experience healed my irrational perception of brokenness. I learned that pain and brokenness is an equal opportunity employer and doesn't discriminate. Our group included all races, all income levels, all types of personalities and all types of body shapes and sizes. The group was truly an enlightening and revelatory experience. Breakthrough

One Saturday night, during an impromptu assignment, we had to participate in a talent show to release our hidden talents. "Oh, my God, I don't sing, dance, etc.…what am I going to do"? Sweetly, the same voice that has been there for me ALL of my life said, Recite Psalms 23, but give the insight that I have given you while you are healing.

While healing, He was using the beautiful imagery in Psalms 23, a holistic scripture, to minister to the broken hearted professors, doctors, lawyers, nurses, teachers etc., to address the trichotomy or three-fold composition of all mankind and their needs. Physical Needs - The Lord is my shepherd, I shall not want. Emotional Needs - He restoreth my soul;--Yea though I walk through the valley…. The light I walk in today is the result of the darkness I've walked through in the valley yesterday…and Spiritual Needs - thou anointest my head with oil; my cup runneth over…broken pieces that I left in the valley have postured and positioned me to live in a newer and higher dimension of holiness. Holiness is holistic. Its vivid imagery expresses emphatically, that since the Lord is our shepherd we don't have any lack.

Depression is a natural part of the process of restoration and we are better, wiser people afterwards if we get something out of this brief season. We have the abundant life and live without fear of the past worries and future anxieties and cares. Brokenness through the valley leads the way to abundance. Breakthrough

During the group experience, one of the group members encouraged me to sell cookies to improve our financial situation. We lived on $250 a month. She showed me an article about two woman who were in similar situations as we were in, where two husbands left their wives and children. The one wife baked and sold chocolate chip cookies for ten cents apiece and the other wife started a catering business selling Italian dinners from her home.

My girlfriend, Regina Powdrill-Davis Shawnie's other godmother, gave me a recipe for chocolate chip butterscotch nut cookies, and also mailed $25.00 in order to start the business. She never questioned me nor made me feel ashamed. She's is a kind, supportive friend and has always been for us for the past sixty plus years.

Miraculously, the saints at church, the family in Detroit, and the group members loved the cookies. We filled orders for three years. I really desired to return the car, a brand new 1978 Ford Fairmont, to Ford Motor Credit, when the Lord said, "I want to make you a witness to my Glory." Indeed He did just that. He touched Daddy's heart for a few months to pay several car notes, then He touched Butch's heart for a few months, then Vocational Rehabilitation paid three car notes.

One influential school principal in the community yelled, "A bag lady with a Master's Degree, selling cookies. What a shame!"

Hurt and embarrassed, I stopped selling for a few days until a young woman in the counseling group ordered 1000 cookies for the annual Ann Arbor Street Fair. That was an honor. I called the local health department for instructions and typed labels for my products. With that large order, I made the final payments on the car and never forgot the kindness of the Lord and how he touched people's hearts. That built some confidence until two more pieces of the shell were restored. Yet, I have not seen the righteous forsaken, nor his seed begging bread." Breakthrough

The most profound experience is when God revealed the masks that we wear that originated in The Fall of Mankind, in the Garden of Eden. Literally it was during the group therapy retreats that God reveal the foundational principles of Inner Healing. The false belief that I must meet certain standards in order to feel ok about myself was based on performance identity which was just as wrong as Eve eating the fruit from the tree of good and evil. The intrinsic belief that I am flawed and don't measure up is a false belief rooted in a lie. God's solution is Justification, just as if I'd never sinned. I was complete in Jesus Christ, and fully pleasing to God. Christ died for all of us while we were yet sinners and this free gift cannot be earned, deserved or paid for. Our proper response is humility and gratitude.

Fear of rejection was the false belief that I must have the approval of significant others to feel good about myself was another lie. This fear motivated shame, people pleasing, codependent behaviors, isolation and withdrawal. But God's solution was Reconciliation, I am reconciled back to God and fully approved. I am accepted and have fellowship with God forever. God sees us perfect. We have incalculable value of the soul.

The fear of condemnation is the false belief that those who fail are unworthy of love and deserve punishment. This lie motivates self-depreciating talk, self-induced punishment, the blame game, bitterness and unforgiveness. God's solution is Propitiation, I am completely forgiven because Jesus Himself became the sacrifices for my wrongdoing and the debt is paid in full.

The fear of not being understood or accepted is the false belief that no one understands or accepts me is a lie. It motivates feelings of loneliness, a sense of hopelessness, isolation, withdrawal from others, and self-pity and a victim mentality. God's solution is Regeneration. I am a new creation in Christ. Jesus came to identify and empathize with us. Breakthrough

During our final group sessions, the psychologist held a graduation ceremony at the end of our retreat. Daddy dropped in unexpectedly. Surprised, I was beginning to finally realize my father's love for me after all these years. He could only give what he had and couldn't give what he never received.

We sat and had a long discussion. I told him how all the fights when we were children affected my love for him and developed a fear of men in me. I said, "How confusing it was to hear you tell me I could be anything I wanted to be, then watch you mistreat Mama." I told him, "No child wants to see their mother hurt."

And I also expressed the double messages that were confusing. I expressed how his sarcasm, even though it was designed to motivate me, simply devastated me. I took it as a put down. I told him all the pressure to receive good grades was setting me up to be a perfectionist, but studies now show that colleges are realizing that perhaps a person with all A's alone is not as balanced and intelligent as they thought because everyone needs to look for balance in all areas of life.

I told him how it seemed as though he favored Denise as he would say, "Here comes my gal" even though I know he loved me. Favoritism can be extremely painful.

He sat, and for the first time let me talk without wanting to take off his glasses and start yelling and fussing. "You'd tell us to speak up to everyone, but you didn't like us doing it to you. Those are double messages too, Daddy."

I told him how he made promises that he did not keep. I continued, "But in the group sessions they had us get on our knees and say everything we wanted to say to our parents as if they were there and then forgive our parents." I don't want my anger to turn into bitterness. Hebrews 12:15 states, "See to it that no one misses the grace of God and produces no bitterness in your own heart."

"Dad, I just want to say thanks for the opportunity to say it to you, but if I never had the chance, I've already forgiven you. I know that you loved me as best you could. There are no perfect set of parents. You just have children and learn. Thanks for being a good provider, thanks for caring now when I really need you the most. I'm very proud of the strength you had to overcome such a traumatic childhood.

Thanks, Dad. I love you. I will try to make you proud of me, but if I never do, I'll always love you. I will be the best person that God created me to be, and right now I'm not sure what that is, but I will find out no matter how long it takes and then I'll be good at it." That night was the beginning of healing unresolved childhood issues. I am so grateful that our relationship was healed before Dad made his transition on February 10, 2009. Breakthrough- Forgive your parents, yourself and family for their brokenness.

After the group therapy, God literally used a little chipmunk that He told me to name her Cherie, my nickname. Cherie appeared daily outside of my home, and I watched her eat grass, plants and carry her nuts. Later she burrowed holes underground in the evening for shelter and rest, then reappear the next morning. He led me to read Matthew 6:24 – 34, "No man can serve two masters…ye cannot serve God and mammon. Therefore, I want to say unto you, Take no thought for your life, what ye shall drink; nor yet for your body, what ye shall put on. Is not the life more than meat, and the body than raiment? Behold the fowls of the air: for they sow not, neither do they reap, nor gather into barns; yet your heavenly Father feedeth them. Are ye not much better than they? But seek ye first the kingdom of God, and his righteousness; and all these things shall be added unto you. Take no thought for the morrow: for the morrow shall take thought for the things of itself. Sufficient unto the day is the evil thereof." This passage clearly deals with a daily cure for anxiety, worry, fret, distress, tension, irritability and uneasiness. Breakthrough

Attending Vic Tanny's Health Spa provided the piece of the shell needed to walk again. My friend, Ann Weaver, now Ann Davis, drove me to and from the facility as I attended daily to assist me as they worked on rebuilding the strength in my legs. Many times the instructor said," Kick your legs in the water and, kick, kick to release the anger and leave it there." Breakthrough

While riding the exercise bike at high speed, I rode over fears, frustrations and anxieties. Lifting weights released heavy burdens. Another piece of the shell was restored. I Thessalonians 5:23, "And the very God of peace sanctify you wholly; and I pray God your whole spirit and soul and body be preserved blameless unto the coming of our Lord Jesus Christ." Breakthrough

The Visiting Nurse came every week and brought with her another piece of the shell. She weighed and checked vital signs. She also taught nutrition and charted caloric intake. I gradually was able to eat solids and drink a protein drink. We talked about the Lord. I learned how to adjust activities, increase rest, decrease certain foods and social activities during irregular cycles and PMS. Foods affect our moods. Breakthrough

The Young Ministers' chairman, Elder Harry Grayson, now, Bishop Harry Grayson, used great wisdom. I was unable to fulfill the responsibilities as the Young Ministers' secretary and desired to resign, but he refused the resignation and encouraged me to maintain my position as he used other team members to assist me until I recovered.

Floyd challenged me with shock therapy; a harsh confrontation. He stated, Carolyn, his late wife, will attempt to do her best at whatever she is called to do. "You have even greater abilities and you won't even try. You deny us of the privilege of receiving the beautiful ministry that only you can share. You are like Moses, offering one excuse after another." Others can be less gifted and talented, but have a greater belief system and will accomplish more for God's Glory.

Just like God, He used Evangelist Yvonne Hawkins as she preached a message the next day about Moses and all of his excuses which means nothing to God, confirming that he was talking to me through Elder Floyd Walton. Breakthroughs

Evangelist Ivy Caddell filled my mind with faith and forgiveness every day. She gave me written prayers for everything from gaining weight to happiness.

The church can begin overcoming the stigma by talking about Mental Illness in their pulpits weekly. There are seven strategies from the acronym teacher that is helpful by Stephen Grcevich, MD, author of Mental Health and The Church.

T: Assemble your inclusion team.
E: Create welcoming ministry environments
A: Focus on ministry activities most essential for spiritual growth.
C: Communicate effectively
E: Offer Education and support
R: Empower your people to assume responsibility for ministry.

Too many people think that being overwhelmed, dealing with depression and such is only a spiritual issue, and that if a person simply prayed and read their Bible more it would go away. Nothing could be further from the truth. Mental illness is a serious issue that the church must be willing to address with compassion, not condemnation. Typically, we criticize and attack what we do not understand. I believe that if the church were more willing to try to understand the reality of mental illness, many people could be helped."

Today our society have more therapists, counselors, psychologists, social workers, psychiatrists and many degreed Mental Health workers yet statistics are recording increases in suicides and opioid addictions in epidemic numbers. I attended a workshop on Resilience in Adverse Childhood Experiences (ACE) which indicates multiple risks factors that contributes greatly to the epidemic. Yet, the answer to the adversities these children experienced is just one loving, caring Christian who is consistently loving and supportive, much like the collective love that we received, who can disciple you to live an abundant life.

"It's more important to receive help from caring, Christian, spiritual people who have the time and ability to listen and direct us into a sustained presence of God than to get the help offered by religious imbalanced Christians who further increase the damage and emotional pain. When sufferers are faced with unskillful leaders and counselors it creates guilt and places the hurting sufferers to learn how to fake their healing for years to remain in the church, or leave the church believing that God doesn't love nor heal emotional problems or mental illnesses. It makes you feel isolated when you see the church members embrace and support the members with physical illnesses and ignore those with mental illnesses." Dr. Stephen Grcevich

We, as leaders must learn from Jesus example in St. John 1:14."….full of grace and truth." I am no longer impressed by any leader who can quote and memorize the scriptures and preach people into a frenzy, but they have no compassion. Neither was my compassion effective without following through with the truth, because I didn't want to hurt their feelings. We must extend undeserved kindness, just as we have received unmerited favor from God. There is an order set in this scripture that requires grace, kindness and compassion first, then deposit the harsh truth that they have denied for years. I would suggest that leaders take a course in Listening and ACE Resilience.

Last, but not least, the spiritual component of healing provided the majority of the pieces of the shell. After gaining enough strength, my friends sent me by train to Longview, Texas to receive counseling from District Elder Noel Jones. After that I visited Youngstown every six months, to receive counseling from District Elder Norman L. Wagner and Indianapolis, Indiana twice to receive counseling from Evangelist Mildred Boyd. In James 5:16, "The effectual fervent prayers of a righteous man availeth much." Breakthrough

During the five day visit, Elder Noel Jones, now Bishop Noel Jones, counseled me daily. He once recommended that I read "The Total Worth of a Woman" by Iverna Tompkins, which was very helpful. He shared very practical things to do to overcome depression. "Change your hairdo, laugh daily, don't take yourself too seriously, and spend more time in recreation.

"You are already devoting tremendous time, energy and effort to strengthening your spirit, now spend more time balancing the soul and the body. Increase your nutritional intake in spite of your loss of appetite."

His Sunday morning message was, Fight. He taught me that as Christians we can become too passive if we rely on prayer alone. We must learn how to pray and fight in spiritual warfare. We must not fight people nor ourselves, but it's important to discern the spirit that motivates the person. Ephesians 6:10-12, concludes that we really don't wrestle at all, but we are commanded to stand on our circumstances, that's the real fight, standing. Breakthrough

During the evening Bible class, a revelatory lesson was taught on hope. Proverbs 13:12, "Hope deferred maketh the heart sick, but when the desire cometh it is a tree of life." My hope was that my husband would provide for us and make us happy. My hope had been displaced and misdirected. The only hope is in Jesus. He was actually the one providing all of our needs; when Benny left us, the hopes for happiness left temporarily, but we learned how to be content and joyful. We were more prosperous with less money. We learned that happiness can be fleeting if we depend on happenings, events and others to fill us, but no one can ever steal our joy and hope in Jesus. Breakthrough

Several family members, saints and friends provided for us.

The Loved Shell

Restoration, katartizo defined means healing, repairing, restoring, mending broken hearts and setting broken bones. Restoration also means to align or put something or someone back in its proper position. Alignment increases your authority to function in the Kingdom of God. Restoration is to receive back more than what has been lost to the point where the final state is greater than the original condition. Someone who is improved beyond measure, before the fall. Repeatedly through the Bible, God blesses people for their faith and hardships by making up for their losses and giving them more than they previously had before, like Job who received double for his trouble.

It is more than mending broken hearts and bringing closure to sad chapters in life; it is refusing to surrender Heaven's best workers to the devil. Therefore, restoration is deploying wounded soldiers (restored) into constructive service for the glory of God as I went forward. One of the ten lepers was healed as he went forward in the process. I entered the process of working in the kingdom of God helping and serving others while healing myself. Synonyms for restoration are renewal, recovery, make you perfect, establish, strengthen and settle you. I Peter 5:10, "But the God of all grace, who hath called us unto his eternal glory by Christ Jesus, after that ye have suffered a while, make you perfect, stablish, strengthen, settle you."

Restoration involves the healing and reconciliation of breaches in relationships.

There is a love that heals damaged emotions. Thanks be to God, that my frozen emotions were thawing out and I finally began to feel loved. My family and church demonstrated the most powerful principle in the Bible, "unconditional love." Matthew 22:37-39, "Jesus said unto him, thou shalt love the Lord thy God with all thy heart, and with all thy soul, and with all thy mind. This is the first and great commandment. And the second is likened unto it. Thou shalt love thy neighbor as thyself. St. John 13:34-35, "A new commandment I give unto you, that ye love one another; as I have loved you, that ye also love one another. By this shall all men know that ye are my disciples, if ye have love one to another?" Breakthroughs

My baby brother, oops, younger brother, Rex K., came to visit from college while he was attending Michigan State University. He wasn't born during the heart of domestic violence in our home, but he experienced some of it. He said, "Cheryl, you're my oldest sister. You left home when I was young, and even though I spent some weekends with you and Benny, he didn't seem to like me because he said I was sarcastic. But I feel like Shawnie is my little sister, not my niece, and you're my big sister and whatever I can do to help you, I will. Here is a poem I bought you about life's challenges. Just get well Sis, I love you."

The Poem: YOU CAN IF YOU THINK YOU CAN
If you think you are beaten...you are!
If you think you dare not....you don't!
Success begins with your own will
It's all in your state of mind.
Life's battles are not always won
By those who are stronger and faster;
And sooner or later, the person who
Wins, is the person who thinks he can!
- Anonymous

I cried when my brother gave me that poem because it showed so much love from the baby. He'd always received so much, but he had learned to give back. I posted it in my bedroom and read it daily for years. Breakthrough

Mama and Daddy both came to visit and said, "Why are you surprised that we would come to check on you? We love you, and whatever you need, we are here. How much money do you need to get caught up? We took some of our savings to help you. Here."

Butch said when he came to visit," Did you ever think so many people would spend so much money trying to be thin like you? I have to exercise every day and pay all this money to the health spa and some people would give anything to be your size. Don't worry so much. I think you should realize that we are an average-looking family and quit getting these fine, light skinned men and get someone who is average, nice and pleasant to be with. You could get married again and be happy like the rest of us." Breakthroughs

Darrell made great financial sacrifices to provide food, cars, car repairs and clothing. He was a gifted mechanic and eventually promoted on his job to a salaried, white collar quality control engineer. Our relationship was significantly healed.

My in laws/love were fantastic! Chally and now Lorita, Saun, Terry and now Alex, Marcy (Dr. G.) and Victor (at the time). Breakthroughs

Attending Eastern Michigan University during that time, I registered for a graduate class, "Counseling for Self-Concept." In the class were high school counselors, principals, teachers and administrators.

The course required an extensive presentation on Building Self-Concept. The challenge was great, as I remembered a statement

District Elder Wagner made, "Return to the last fear and conquer it." The classroom was my last fear. Being faced with this challenge was overwhelming.

The Lord instructed me to fast and pray for three days. I was obedient, and when it was time for the presentation, I depended on the Lord to speak through me, He did. They were left spellbound as God taught the lesson through me on the spiritual aspect of holistic esteem and being complete in Him. Colossians 2:10, "And, ye are complete in him, which is the head of all principality and power:" Breakthrough

During the course of the two years, the most of the shell was repaired, restored and strengthened. The Lord took several of His vessels to put me back together again. Then I made a vow, that I will give back to others what they have given to me by helping other people in my situation. Salvation was the initial onetime event. The continual learning process of the principles of repentance, brokenness, restoration, skills and tools in transformation and maintenance, are essential to experience total deliverance.

The holistic method of integration is very effective. Integrating biblical truths and biblically-based psychological principles, as well as nutrition, rest and physical exercise developed discipline, a Godly image, esteem and worth.

Small success led to greater successes and risk taking. The torment and stronghold of fear was dissipating. I no longer had a fear of failure or of success.

Meditating on the Word of God for fifteen minutes a day quieted my mind while; exercising for six months provided more confidence as well as a relaxed body. Learning to overcome stress was essential. My Vocational Rehabilitation counselor closed my case. The shell restored.

Unconditional love is powerful. It is the highest form of God's love with an unconditional regard for the welfare of another, while maintaining one's own self-love.

While watching others love me, and yet never neglecting their own worth, I finally understood that the love we were taught as children was conditional and had its origin in materialism and humanism. I used the wrong value system to measure my worth. Love and forgiveness is healing.

You will never be free until you FORGIVE. Forgiveness is not a feeling, but an act of your will, choosing to surrender the hurt to God and trusting Him enough to heal you. We make the choice and God makes the change.

One day during a forgiveness exercise in prayer, I identified different people in my life who I needed to forgive. The longer I prayed, the longer the list became. I realized then that I was harboring a lot of unforgiveness. I even went way back to my second grade teacher, who gave me a U for unsatisfactory. I was afraid because we were only allowed to bring home E's for excellence. I realized then that I'd held grudges for years. No wonder I was sick. Colossians 3:13, "Forbearing one another, and forgiving one another, if any man have a quarrel against any: even as Christ forgave you, so also do ye." Breakthrough

Holistic healing required that you learn lessons from the past to become familiar with your strengths and weaknesses and use them to grow. I thanked the Lord for using everyone I encountered as a teacher in life. I was also thankful that the Lord didn't allow me to continue living with ungodly thoughts. Forgiveness is a daily process.

I realized what I thought was love was a misconception. True love does not hurt or harm you, misuse or abuse you, nor deceive you or string you along. Love is action. The two marriages I had with the same man were not real love. Relationships that irk and jerk your emotions are either seasonal, and have reached their expiration date, or are very toxic. Let them go.

The fourth step in wholeness is restoration. God restored me back to the original me, before the foundation of the world. Just because I had a broken heart didn't mean that I was a broken person. Psalms 51:12 states, "Restore unto me the joy of thy salvation; and uphold me with thy free spirit."

He restored my purpose, to improve the quality and longevity of life by supporting others as described in Galatians 6:1-3. We help restore others while they are carrying a heavy burden, and at an appointed time we allow them to grow by accepting their responsibility to carry their own burden. I was called to please God. With a new set of values and lessons in life, I had an opportunity for on-the-job training.

Had I really learned all that I needed to change, to be transformed into the image of Jesus Christ? It took years for me to learn the transformation process and new ways of living by the renewing of the mind. Whatever is not transformed becomes transferred. You are destined to live your history unless you change it to the predesigned destiny of God. Romans 12:2 “Be not conformed to this world, but be ye transformed by the renewing of your mind.” Breakthrough

SECTION THREE
THE WORK

CHAPTER 5
MOVING FROM EGYPT TRANSFORMATION IN CANAAN, THE PROMISED LAND

God will often transition us to transform us. God was repositioning us, because we are always headed somewhere in His momentum. Arriving at our new destination requires change. For most of us, change creates stress, whether it's eustress (good) or distress (bad). Life is filled with many transitions (moving from one place to another) from the womb to the tomb; from the cradle to the first day entering kindergarten; from grade school to high school; from high school to the military, college, ministry or career; from a military, college, ministry or career to marriage; from marriage to parenthood; from parenthood to retirement; from retirement to mentoring; from mentoring and leisure time to the rapture or death.

During those transitions, we can get trapped in negativity without the proper direction and training for living life. "Life is a gift, but living is an art form." NLW. Some individuals who suffer in silence with treated mental health issues within the church according to Dr. Kevin K. Daniels, are in their finest hour. God has postured them to be used greatly because of their minds ability and experiences with mental health issues. However, there must be prepared ministries to minister, guide and counsel these individuals to live in higher dimensions of thinking, otherwise those individuals will revert back to living in their emergencies rather than living in their emerging call. In other words he stated they will live in their pathology, rather than live in their possibilities without the proper counsel. I am a witness that the Lord, God Almighty will transform us if we are willing to yield to the long, slow process of sanctification and transformation. The ministry of Inner Healing is really not for a few troubled souls, but it is a vital key to the transformation of every heart of a normal Christian we all have areas that need to be transformed.

Transformation is proceeded by brokenness and is the process of death and rebirth whereby what was our weakness becomes our strength. Inner Healing shifts us from merely looking back at our pasts and attempting to correct our self-image. Inner Healing transforms us and catapults us beyond our Adamic sin nature. The Adamic sin-nature is the motivation for our wrong choices and behaviors and our spirit transforms us into the Biblical revelation of Godly motivations from the heart. God will remove the band aids that were covering the gaping holes, breaches wounds and pain. God is opening the door for the sanctification and transformation to the entire body of Christ to heal from all the wounds incurred from life's transitions, whether it is healing spiritually, financially, emotionally, or physically. He transforms us.

If I wanted to feel better I had to learn to think better and perceive life through the lens of God. Our healing as Christians doesn't come by God taking our broken places, patching us up and making us good enough to work. No, but by delivering us from the power of that broken thing so it can no longer rule us. He teaches us to trust His righteousness to shine in and through the light of the breaks and cracks. God heals by leaving the broken part right there in place, and overcoming it by His nature. God uses broken things for His glory instead of rebuilding personal pride and confidence in the flesh.

Romans 12:2, "And be not conformed to this world, but be ye transformed by the renewing of your mind, that ye may prove what is that good, and acceptable, and perfect will of God." Transformation is an inward change that built us up on the inside enabling us to live from the "inside out" drawing our worth and values from the Holy Ghost living on the inside of us. It adjusts the mind, and consequently, adjusts our lives permanently to the Word of God. We adjust our minds to the mind of Christ and posture ourselves daily to be tested so that we have yielded to God in order to prove that the Word of God has changed us. Our faith becomes relevant because it demonstrates the evidence that cannot be denied that our lives have changed or been transformed.

Therefore, I become the witness that testifies to the undeniable fact that I've been changed by the love that God has for me. I have been reconciled back to Him through the sacrifice of Jesus Christ, our redeemer. Now that God helped me identify the source of my strongholds, I was learning how to isolate the lies and replace them with God's truth.

With a fresh start, being debt free, healthy and restored, the psychologist agreed that it was time to secure a part-time job, gradually working toward working full-time.

The Ypsilanti Board of Education Adult Education Division offered me a part-time position as a Business Education Teacher earning ten dollars an hour, twenty hours a week. Shawnie earned three-hundred dollars that summer and purchased her entire wardrobe as she eagerly awaited her first year at Ypsilanti High School. Suddenly the voice that had spoken to me for years, gave life-changing directives.

As I was packing to attend the summer young people's convention in Milwaukee, Wisconsin the Lord said, "Don't attend the convention. While all your friends are away, pack your townhouse from top to bottom. On Sunday, August 21, 1983, I want you to attend Mt. Calvary and visit there five days."

Following directives, I planned the trip with two couples, Elder and Sister Michael Cannon and the late Brother and Sister Art Williams, who loved to visit Youngstown. During that Sunday service, the pivotal message that changed my life was "Gateway to the Morning." District Elder Wagner stated, "...though the Holy Ghost has come everything is new but their mind. They have to learn to adopt the mind of Christ...unless someone knows deliverance they will not stay saved...what we do about a struggling soul who can't seem to find Him. I've got the answer:

"In the year that King Uzziah died, I saw the Lord. Everything that represents control and ruler ship in your life must die...your spirit must reject what your mind knows because your mind was educated by man, but your spirit will bring you up and out...when I stopped trusting in the arms of flesh...you're not here by accident. If God doesn't bless you this week, my name won't be what it is…" There again is the beginning of my process of death and rebirth. I was about to learn that nothing in our lives is ever wasted and transformation is a slow process.

The two couples returned to Michigan. I stayed in Youngstown. Within five days Calvary Christian Academy of Higher Learning principal, Arnold Wagner, unexpectedly offered me a position as a Social Studies and Psychology Teacher. I turned to District Elder Wagner for counsel before returning to Michigan. That was an unforgettable Wednesday evening. While sitting in his office he said, "The decision is yours. You are a butterfly in a cocoon. You are about to fly. Whether you fly in Youngstown or you fly in Ypsilanti, you are going to fly!"

The caterpillar's metamorphosis provides a wonderful illustration of a born-again believer's spiritual transformation. When the caterpillar feeds on the leaves or ideas of the world around us, it's at its lowest infant, immature stage. When the caterpillar changes its form into a pupa or chrysalis it's synonymous to being born again as it dies out from the world and sin and develops into the spiritual realm being. When the butterfly is in the cocoon, it's dark and hanging upside down, but eventually breaks through the hardness of the shell and emerges from his/her cocoon. It (he/she) flies, something it (he/she) couldn't do before. The butterfly also drinks sweet nectar instead of gorging on leaves. It (he/she) never returns back to its (his/her) old ways or appearances ever again. It (he/she) receives it's breakthrough to a new life, touches lives with its beauty everywhere it flies as a sign of growth, maturity and change. Likewise, I looked forward to my breakthrough to the new me.

No one knew about the butterfly's significance to my transformation except the Lord and close friends. How in the world could Elder Wagner know this? I discerned this man of God knew the Lord in a way that the average saint didn't. I felt led in my spirit that the time had come to move to Youngstown. I said yes, but I had great fights with fear afterwards for a few days. I was still moving forward, but returned home still seeking the Lord for final confirmation.

While waiting on the final answer from the Lord, my sister shared the message the Lord gave her, "Follow Me." Minister Henry Frost preached on Friday night Young People's service from Joshua 1:1-9 and entitled his sermon, "The Challenge." I surrendered to Sovereign control, only the Lord God Himself is in control. During that time, still seeking confirmations within that time frame, several people unknowingly confirmed our move to Youngstown. I needed to know beyond a shadow of a doubt. Life was really, really comfortable for us, so why move now, I thought? Why Now? Well the answer came immediately.

The following Sunday, while traveling to Detroit to accompany Evangelist Yvonne Hawkins who was the guest minister at New Creation, pastored by the late Bishop Lottie Glynn-Richie, which was the church my sister attended. I noticed she was unusually quiet.

I asked, "Yvonne, do you need me to be quiet?"

Her response was, "Yes, I'm wrestling between two messages."

I really wasn't expecting a Word from the Lord through her, she and my other mentors told me to stay home and don't move to Youngstown, because I was still fragile. Yet her message was life changing, "God Needs Somebody Who Will Go?" She preached out of Isaiah 6:1-8 "In the year that King Uzziah died I saw also the Lord sitting upon a throne high and lifted up and His train filled the temple …Also I heard the voice of the Lord saying Whom shall I send and who will go for me? Then Isaiah said, "Here am I; send me." The total essence of her message was that living for Jesus means taking all of life's preparations, lessons, experiences, joys, hurts and pain and at the appointed time, use it as an education as an eyewitness to testify regarding how to overcome our blockages within that cause us to make idols within and idolatry with our spiritual celebrities.

This is the second time I've heard Isaiah's message regarding Isaiah's call to ministry and placed The Lord back on the throne of his heart.

Those who worship the Lord in spirit and in truth do not attend church to sing, shout, socialize and showcase their gifts and talents like they are on parade, and equate these actions with being anointed and saved. Bishop Wagner once ministered a message, Anointed, but Awful; but worship is actually a lifestyle of total obedience. The Truth is, we are attending services for God to reveal hard truths that will dispel satanic lies within us, breakthrough the fallow, hard, unsurrendered and transform lies and ungodly motivations. We are more often than not, moved by our perception based on our five senses of taste, smell, sight, hearing and touch. Living in the spirit goes beyond our perception and emotions, and my heart delights in following Him, wherever He leads me, even when I don't understand. This was another confirmation.

God will always confirm His Word by two or three witnesses. The late Missionary Jones finalized the confirmation concerning my destiny with this prophecy. "Oh, Sister Bass, the Lord is sending you away to do a great work for Him. Look neither to the left nor the right. There will be some suffering, but He will bless you, because you are in His will." That's It! She never knew the decision I was faced with. She attended church fifty miles away. How could she know this? Once again my Lord had spoken. Confirmation had come. It was time to move!

Shocked, I saw it was not only the Lord's perfect will, but His timing. Evangelist Hawkins-Bell, said "I knew when I took my text that God is sending you away. Here read Joshua1 and don't stop until He tells you to stop, I stopped at versus 7, 8 and 9 in awe. Wow "look not to the left nor the right… be of good courage….meditate on the Word day and night and you will have good success." They were similar words God spoke through the prophet, Missionary Jones. My next question, "How am I going to tell Elder Ross that I definitely know it's time for me to move? When I talked to him last Friday, he told me that I could stay here in Ypsilanti, continue to heal, where everyone knows my condition, grow in ministry, then you may move. He won't be too happy with this decision." Confirmation had come. It's imperative that you develop an intimate relationship with the Lord, God and Savior because He speaks directly to you first, then uses vessels to confirm His Word that He revealed to you.

She answered, "Just tell him you know it is God's will and he will know it's the Lord."

When we returned from Detroit for our Sunday evening service, I beckoned to Elder Ross to come out of the pulpit into the basement during the night service. He was such a loving, kind, humble, compassionate pastor.

When I said with tears in my eyes, "I now know it is the Lord's will for me to move to Youngstown. I need your blessings."

He hung his head and said, "Sister Cherie, I'm like a father who hates to lose his daughter. You're my daughter and I'm going to miss you terribly, but I take my hands off of it, because it is the Lord, and you have my blessings to go and serve the people of the Lord."

I cried and hugged him. He was always like a grand-father to me after Grandpa died.

Only seven days remained before accepting the position. In total, I had fourteen days to move, secure residence and begin working. When we shared the news about our decision to move, the phone began to ring night and day as saints, friends and family called, asking; "Is it really true that you are moving?" When I responded yes, they cried over the telephone. I wept for days.

The saints gathered at the house night and day to assist us. Shawnie withdrew and was depressed for several days. I understood what she was experiencing. She didn't want to move and leave her friends. She'd looked forward to attending Ypsilanti High School for several years. In junior high school she was the only saved child, but many saved young people attended Ypsilanti High. She would no longer feel uncomfortable. I remembered promising myself, because of the pain I suffered during my high school transition, moving to a new high school, that I'd never do this to my child. I've learned, never vow what you will never do. You just never know.

Shawnie's needs were great and The Lord was gracious to her in spite of the characteristics that manifested themselves as a result of the codependency, living with drug abuse. He gave her an improved personality in the spirit as long as she stayed in the church. When she decided that she wanted to explore other interests, her old personality returned. I knew that moving to Youngstown was being obedient to God's will and it would be beneficial for both of our personal and spiritual development.

After a farewell party given for us on Friday, September 2, 1983, we left Ypsilanti, Michigan on Sunday, September 4, 1983 with exactly $125.00 to our name in my purse. Min. Carol Hollis drove us to Youngstown and as we crossed the state line the sign read, Welcome, Ohio Loves You.

Immediately, the Lord spoke these unforgettable words, "You have just left your Egypt land filled with pain, tears and suffering and entered your Canaan Land which flows with milk and honey. You will be greatly blessed. "Just as Abraham had to leave his support systems in the land of Ur and move to a new land, a new beginning, likewise your move is to bless you. I will bless those who bless you and curse those who curse you. You will be a great blessing to my people in ministry. You will receive abundant financial blessings. You will marry a good, loving companion. Your daughter will be blessed and I will make up the difference for all of your sacrifices in your life."

Pondering all these promises in my heart, I wrote them in my diary. All these wonderful promises in Canaan Land, Youngstown. In order to live out of the fullness of my new identity in Christ, I had to identify what was hindering me from living the abundant life. What life experiences interfered with me seeing myself as God sees me. I had to live through false beliefs and mistaken identities and transform to the image of Christ from: (1) rejection to acceptance (2) bondage to redemption (3) law to grace – human doings to human beings (4) feeling orphaned to adoption.

I was learning how to be rooted and grounded in Christ. My new identity, my value, importance and worth was based on a higher, heavenly value system. Feeling valuable based on a higher system changed the way I felt about myself and others. When I maintained a sense of mental well-being my decisions were positive and impactful.

It was time to be totally committed to the Lord and sacrifice my comforts. How exciting it was to realize that I would be sitting under the teaching of the man of God that I'd traveled all over the states to hear, preach and teach at National Conventions, church conventions, church anniversaries. You name it, I was there. Many times the services began at 8 o'clock in Detroit, forty minutes from Ypsilanti, but we left and were in service at 5 o'clock just to get a seat since hundreds traveled from far and near to hear what the Lord would say. I envisioned Shawnie and I in his power-packed church and felt we would truly be made whole again.

THE TRANSFORMED SHELL

The fifth step is to develop a renewed mind. Transformation is the change from one form or character into a different form or state or person. It's not an event, but actually a lifetime process of breakthroughs that changes mindsets, one thought after another. In the original Greek language of the New Testament, the word used for transformation is metamorphosis "metamorpho". Although an outward change in appearance or form takes place, the change comes from within the life of an organism. Transformation is not adjusting our behavior to look more like Christ by doing good things or improving our conduct.

Transformation means change or renewal from a life that no longer conforms to the ways of the world, but to a lifestyle and value system in our core belief system that pleases God. Striving for popularity, seeking approval, material possessions, status, control, power, prestige, cliques are carnal and worldly. Setting our affections on prayer, fasting, purpose, and destiny and using gifts to give God glory is pleasing God. This is accomplished by renewing our minds daily with intentional focus in the Word of God, praying, fasting and receiving a new mindset, Christ like thinking which is manifested and reflected by our behaviors. When challenges occur I intentionally choose to respond rather than react emotionally. It's a life time process of learning how to manage, direct and transform my emotions.

When difficulties come I am learning how to automatically view them through the eyes of God's Word. God's reality, His perspective changes everything. Transformation requires a surrender of our self-control to the obedience of the Holy Spirit. Brokenness is God's requirement for usefulness which helped me learn how to live beyond my emotions.

Our move was extremely challenging. It was the turning point to an abundant life, one I'd always dreamed about, prayed about and hoped for. There were ten times the number of people in Mt. Calvary compared to our other church. Young and old from different sections of the nation and some from foreign countries were sent by the Lord to Calvary.

Unable to secure our own home, my daughter and I moved in with a family. Within seven days, we were asked to move out. Sister Alice Carlisle opened her door to us for one month, then the pastor's mother, Sister Louise Wagner, (whom I affectionately called "Roadrunner") kept us for ten days.

One Friday night, after young people's service, I stopped Pastor Wagner to inform him of our dilemma. He said, "When you are in the will of the Lord, He will provide." Where God Guides He Provides.

Shortly afterwards, while looking for housing, a yellow framed house, was illuminated to me and I heard that sweet familiar voice say, "This is your home."

It took several days to contact the owner but her response was, "I'm sorry. Four others have called concerning this apartment. I can't rent it to you unless all four back out which is highly unlikely."

I replied, "The Lord told me this apartment is ours and that you will rent it to us."

Stunned, she said, "The most amazing thing happened. No one else wants to rent this apartment after all. It's yours."

Excited that the Lord manifested himself once more, we moved in. The duplex did not include a stove, refrigerator nor curtains for fifteen empty windows. I wondered, "How am I going to get all these things?" At school, while sharing my problem with the staff, the football coach, Brother Paul Pegues, now Bishop Pegues, said, "Just believe the Lord. We walk by faith not by sight."

Amazed, I told the Lord, "I believe."

Within two days, Mama called and said, "When Aunt Creola died, she left her stove and refrigerator to Butch which he doesn't need. You can have them if you can get the moving company to bring them with the rest of your belongings. Besides, you gave me all your drapes throughout the years so I'm sending you draperies for every window in the house." Aunt Creola? Look at God!

I began to see that faith, my frame of mind and attitude were very important for living a successful, abundant, victorious life. Every new principle I learned had to be applied daily because Shawnie and I were homesick and lonely. Initially, I felt like I was grieving and didn't understand until I read a book, No Longer Lonely, on loneliness which said, "A person usually feels the loneliest after they move from their home to a new city. It feels as though they have buried everyone they've ever loved at the same time." That's exactly how I felt!

Different saints extended themselves to us, Dr. Joyce Phifer, the late Evangelist Saundra Ponzo and her husband, Brother Kenneth, the late Elder Gerald Morgan and his family, Ruby Warren, Belinda Wilson, The Carpenter family and a host of supportive families.

Bible classes were exciting; the services exhilarating. I shouted myself silly. For years I couldn't believe District Elder Norman L. Wagner had now become my pastor. But it was really true. I was not living in a dream, but in his services. He taught a powerful lesson on Katartizo, putting away childish things. I Corinthians 13:11, "When I was a child, I understood as a child, I thought as a child; but when I became a man, I put away childish things." Put away means to render inoperative, or powerless; to remove the meaning or significance from; to free from that which has been keeping one bound or tied up. Remove our faulty beliefs and wrong impressions of my past remove the power from my childhood. He's actually telling us to stop thinking the wrong things about ourselves.

Transforming the lies that kept me captive for years is a daily process. I shifted from the lies to the truth. Learn to identify the lies. I began with the lie of rejection, the first stronghold God revealed to me. The key to victory is to acknowledge and address the root, the lies that I'd been tricked into believing and thinking are true. Examine my behavior after an event to see what I was really thinking. Was I responding with the fruit of the spirit of a new creature in Christ or the fruit of the flesh, the old man? I was guilty of black and white, all or nothing thinking.

10 Types of Negative thoughts and beliefs linked to mental/emotional problems. Please circle the areas you still struggle with.

1. All-or-Nothing Thinking - The person who thinks this way sees everything in black or white. Perfectionist see their work as either perfect or worthless. Healthy people see

spectrums and variations and exceptions in nearly every area of life.

2. Overgeneralizations - The tendency to draw conclusions from little evidence. The healthier person draws conclusions after taking in a great deal of evidence.

3. Negative Mental Filter – This person filters out any bit of information that is positive. They don't hear compliments or affirmations. They only hear criticism. The healthy person hears both the good and the bad.

4. Disqualifying the Positive - This person hears the compliment, but discounts it. They explain away words of affirmation and praise. A healthy person receives compliments and praise and uses them to validate their core belief and value.

5. Jumping to Conclusions - This person believes they know at all times, with 100 percent accuracy, what other people are thinking about them. The healthy person assumes they aren't a mind reader.

6. Magnification or Minimization- This person exaggerates the importance of isolated events or encounters. They may magnify their own emotions, mistakes, or imperfections. They minimize, however, any success they may have. A healthy-thinking person maximizes their good points and minimizes their failures.

7. Emotional Reasoning - This person sees an outcome as directly flowing from their emotions. For example, this person may feel hopeless about passing an exam, so they won't show up to take it. The healthy person separates current feelings from future events, shows up and passes the exam.

8. Should Statements – This person has a rigid set of internal rules about what should be, what must be, what we ought to do, what we can't do, and what has to be done. The

healthy person knows and expresses the fact that there are very few hard-and-fast rules in life.

9. Labeling and Mislabeling – This person is likely to give himself or another person negative labels such as stupid, idiot, imbecile, loser, jerk, or pig. The healthy person avoids labels.

10. Personalization – This person blames himself for events over which he has no control or less control than he assumes. The healthy person sets healthy boundaries and refuses to take responsibility or blame for someone else's freewill choices.

I replaced rejection with affirmation, because rejection makes it difficult to receive positive affirmations. Rejection reduced my core beliefs whereas affirmations fed and built-up my core of who I really am. The spiritual truth is God sees and accepts me. I started breaking free from emotional strongholds when I increased my awareness and changed my thinking, which then changed my behavior in three areas:

1. My greatest need is not self-confidence—it's confidence in God.
2. God uses my difficult experiences to prepare me for future ministry.
3. Obeying God leads to a new, accurate image of myself in Him.

My perception was changing about how I viewed the world and felt about myself and others. Life seemed great. I learned many lessons on Inner Healing. I soon realized that life as a Christian was a spiritual battle and that some suffering did come from within, as well as oppressing spirits that attacked from without. I felt relieved that I wasn't crazy after all, but was involved in periods of self-examination as well as spiritual warfare. Knowing that made it easier to resist those strongholds and evil spirits and yield to the Spirit of the Lord.

A stronghold is a fortress which is used as defenses. They are large walls that are impenetrable. A stronghold is a wrong belief, especially a wrong belief about God. They are reasoning's and arguments and theories that go against God. We give the enemy a stronghold and a right to play havoc in our lives when our thoughts are carnal. Childhood memories are one the greatest source of strongholds, however, our Adamic propensity to sin is the greatest. We learn through a process of time how to put off and put on new spiritual, relational, emotional patterns of thinking. It's imperative to take the creative powers we inherited in our new birth and imagine God as He really is and not allow these strongholds to interfere with our ability to see God. Any misconception we have about God is why we need to be transformed in the very depths of our being. Personally, I once perceived God as a critical, distant, punitive father who only cared about my perfect performance before He'd love me. Well that was a familiar spirit that was transformed before I grew in the grace of God.

Colossians 3:8. My motivation for putting off the old man's way of thinking and putting on the new man's way of thinking was by recognizing whose I was first, then who I am in Him. It wasn't easy, but it was worth it. We, Christians, are a chosen people, holy, and dearly loved according to Colossians 3:12. I had to mature from the old labels and names that were attached to me in the past and embrace the new loving names in my mind and my heart.

Learning to resist old familiar spirits was indeed a warfare. When I felt empty and lonely, because I had no husband or boyfriend, I remembered what Pastor Wagner said, "You're only lonely if you're immature and haven't learned to love yourself. Maturity seeks quiet and solitude as opportunities to get to know yourself and grow. You do not need a crowd of people around you all of the time. Too many voices can distract you from listening to God."

When the familiar spirit of depression showed his ugly head I had to learn to use the art of self-talk as King David did in Psalms 42:5 and ask, "Soul, why art thou cast down, hope thou in God?" I talked to myself and said, "Cheryl, did you forget you have a God who loves you?" I had to learn how to help myself instead of depending on other people. The revelation that the spirit of depression manifests itself in our family for several generations, motivated me to embrace the lessons while going through this depressed season to improve the quality of my life. Self-talk is very important for our healing.

During a pity-party or a slump I'd say, "Nobody is receiving an invitation to your poor me party. Stop it right now! Get up from here because nobody is coming! This party is over!" Self-pity is the stance of a victim where they perceive that things have been done to them. They want to place blame but don't want help and boast in one's suffering. It is a must to recognize we are only giving our power away. Take back our responsibility.

I learned to talk to myself in Godly, positive, healthy ways. The more spiritual the conversation, the better and healthier I felt both emotionally and physically. I no longer spent as many hours in bed, but actually began enjoying spending time alone with the Lord in meditation and contemplative prayer when transforming emotions.

I often wondered how I would be able to minister when I was asked to minister at Calvary, because of their exceptional ministry and congregation of two-thousand members. When I was fearful while learning to preach at Messias Temple the congregation was two hundred members. My hands were sweaty, legs were shaky, and I struggled to speak with my soft, squeaky voice. However, I'd meditate on Timothy 1:7, "But God hath not given us the spirit of fear, but of love, power and of a sound mind." Sometimes I repeated it a hundred times a day. I imagined a glass full of fear and began emptying it, and filling it with faith. It was also necessary to visualize the place and the people, where I was to speak, with me standing calmly before them on a platform that God built.

The spirit of inferiority challenged me often, but I quoted Saint Luke's gospel 17:21: "...the Kingdom of God is within me, and Philippians 4:13, "I can do all things through Christ which strengthens me."

At times, when I was exhausted, I depended on Acts 17:28 to be energized: "In Him we live and move and have our being." Often times the spirit of worry caused me wonder about our future. Then I quoted Philippians 4:6 "Be careful for nothing but in everything through prayer and supplication with thanksgiving let your request be made known unto God."

During times that logic and irrational thoughts tried to overtake me, I meditated on Proverbs 3:5-6," Trust in the Lord with all thine heart and lean not unto thine own understanding. In all thy ways acknowledge him and he shall direct my paths." And Corinthians 10: 4-5, "Casting down strongholds...and bringing into captivity every thought to the obedience of Jesus Christ."

I noticed a great change in the way I handled anger. Instead of allowing the fury and fire to be turned inward, I was able to acknowledge that I was angry and used assertive confrontational skills, rather than become a victim. Read Ephesians 4, especially versus 25-31. This passage will teach you how to get along and love people you don't like. Sadly, it took decades for me to learn that everyone isn't going to like me, or one another, but we are commanded to love.

I think that the unrealistic expectations from people is one of the greatest tricks and distractions of the adversary. When I was expecting that everyone in the church was going to like me because we're saved, I was inflicting myself with unrealistic wounds. God sorely corrected me and taught me how to shift my focus back to Jesus Christ and not to myself and others. Our purpose is to make the world look more like the Kingdom of God each day. I had to empty myself of the pride that was driving my desire to be accepted by everyone. Realize that it is impossible for you or me to gain everyone's approval, but commit to pleasing God. As a Christian we are sharing in the sufferings of Christ as a privilege. As a Christian you will experience rejection, just as Jesus did as a man. I am not exempt from being rejected in daily life.

His requirement from me was that I loved Him and myself enough to allow Him to love others through me. I was to respond to them in love and not react. I learned to manage my expectations of people and embrace relationships that celebrate and release controlling relationships to Him.

If individuals chose not to speak to me, they have actually made a decision that they don't really feel like speaking to themselves and I respond in love, not react in hurt. Our behavior and interaction with one another also reflects the relationship we have with God. Everyone's motivations in life will eventually be revealed.

God's reality is that I was called as a single woman into ministry. Even when I shared my desire to remarry because I wanted to have two more children, Pastor Wagner kept instructing me, "Get involved in ministry, and serve the people in love. Everything else is secondary." Seek God first.

Ministry became my focus for one year. I organized a team of twelve people from Calvary and we traveled to Ypsilanti for a weekend of ministry and fellowship. We taught seminars and preached. The Lord anointed the team we called "Unity". Excited, we planned to travel to various cities, ministering to others.

When I began to work on my ministerial license, all the demons from the pit must've decided to attack me. I remembered the words of Missionary Jones, "Keep your eyes straight ahead on Jesus and your pastor. Do not look to the left nor the right."

I wanted to be obedient and do right, but something stopped me. Once again, I struggled with my emotions which are powerful. Failing to heed the directions, I began regressing, rather than progressing. I was tired of being lonely and started developing unhealthy emotional, not sexual, male relationships over a four-year-period, because I felt they needed me. God kept me virtuous from the end of my marriage to Benny for ten years, even when I didn't want to be kept virtuous.

What isn't transformed will be transferred. Even though I had the gifts of listening and compassion I didn't know how to operate them, so returned to my old behaviors. I tried again to be a rescuing savior, and thought it was really God's will. I needed to learn how to discern the difference between rescuing, enabling relationships and showing genuine compassion like Jesus.

One relationship after another left me emotionally drained, until one day Pastor Wagner counseled me and said, "You are anointed. The danger in being anointed is the anointing draws people to you. They don't always understand it is the anointing they see, not you. Then they proceed to draw off your anointing like a leach, suck you dry and leave you burnt out. In some cases they then have your anointing which leaves you empty, broken and wounded. Then the Lord has to heal you again. Guard your heart. Protect it."

I finally learned the lesson that broke that stronghold of emotional dependencies that I am still learning, but much more mature. One day I'd experienced emotional and physical abuse in the worst way. I read, "Women Who Love Too Much", is a book by Robin Norwood. I finally saw the error of my ways! Amazed at the profile, I quickly recognized my life in those pages. I asked the Lord, "What can I do to be genuine. Help me!"

Some statements which gave insight were the excerpts that stated why women who love too much stay in painful and dissatisfying relations. They stay because they believe that is the way all intimate relationships are supposed to be. Therefore these women become obsessed with their relationships. I read where loving can be too much when a partner is inappropriate, uncaring or unavailable. Yet I saw myself as one who couldn't give mine up. In fact, I felt I needed him more than ever. That yearning became an addiction.

The author even cited an example of my childhood, and stated "Parents are fighting, the child feels afraid and the child asks mother, "Why are you mad at Daddy?" Mother answers, "I'm not mad," while looking angry and troubled. This child now feels confused, more afraid, and says, "I heard you shouting." Mother replies angrily. The child feels fear, confusion, anger, and guilt. Her parent has implied that her perceptions are incorrect, but if that is true, where are these feelings of fear coming from? The child must now choose between knowing that she is right and that her parent has deliberately lied to her, or thinking that she is wrong in what she hears, sees, and feels. She will often settle for confusion, tuning out her perceptions so that she does not have to experience the discomfort of having them invalidated.

This impairs a child's ability to trust herself and her perceptions, both in childhood and later in adulthood, especially in close relationships." I suffered for decades with doubt in my heart.

I screamed, "Oh, Dear God, that's it! That's what's wrong with me! I finally faced the truth about myself. I'm addicted to abuse, just like Benny was addicted to heroin. Please help me Jesus!" That same week, at my daughter's open house, Elder Paul Moore called me to the side and said, "The Lord loves you and has a great anointing on your life and a blessed ministry. Go on in your ministry. I love you like you are my sister. I don't want you to miss all that the Lord has for you."

"Perhaps you've just been lonely and vulnerable in different situations, and if you are afraid tell Pastor, but please let go."

Two days later, Pastor's Sunday morning message was, "Returning to Egypt" He said, "The Lord has brought you out of Egypt, but you are returning to your captivity. If you do not turn, your families will die and be destroyed." I thanked the Lord for His mercy and longsuffering. I experienced pain for a while, but the Lord began to fill my void Himself, just trust Him.

The breaking point caused me to face myself and realize that I must change, I was in transitory places trying to make them permanent places, and I needed to learn life skills for permanent change.

Friends were like mirrors who encouraged me to see myself the way God does. They presented an image of myself that I didn't recognize. Their feedback was powerful because the entire ministry at Calvary is based on personal development of the young and old. Everyone has a place and they helped direct me to mine, when I was totally unaware of how blessed I really was.

Finally the realization hit full force. No one could do what I had to do for the Lord, but me! I was unique in Him and valuable. I finally unveiled my entire humanness without the masks, the facade, the fake smile and the veneer of confidence. I came empty, dependent solely on the Lord, yet willing to be obedient and do whatever He told me. No more fear, no more selfish ambitions nor drives of the flesh. My only desire was to be the minister who the Lord wanted me to be.

Prestige, material possessions, relationships, popularity, degrees, nothing else must come before the desire to serve my Jesus.

The Lord immediately opened doors. The very next week He blessed me to minister in a five day revival and seminar presentation to the Single Sisters and entire congregation in Akron, Ohio.

"The fifth message preached was, "Broken to be Made Whole." The Lord spoke to me once again in the preparation of the five messages and told me the nights and the order in which to preach them. He even had me change the scripture that He usually gives me for the message in Saint Matthew 5:3 dealing with the multitude of broken people, to Daniel 4, using Nebuchadnezzar. He told me one specific, anointed, unbroken person who would be at the church that night and that he had a specific warning of judgment for that person.

He stated, "Just like Nebuchadnezzar, they are mighty and great, but pride has caused them to be blinded by their sins. I am going to bring them down like Nebuchadnezzar if they do not turn (repent), but I will raise them up again. You are to pray for them regardless of what happens. Believe me and watch me work a divine miracle."

Changing the message and preaching it as the Lord directed, I was very nervous that night. But just as the Lord had stated, the soul came and heard the word. That person was hewn down on their face and eventually restored back to their place in the kingdom as an anointed vessel.

Many doors were opened afterwards for ministry. Teaching at Calvary Christian Academy was also a ministry. The Lord directed me to close the history books for one week and teach the students a series of lessons entitled, "I Am Somebody Because I'm God's Body." He said, "Take the students into the sanctuary with three written requests. The power of God fell on the entire student body. There were twelve students that left home unsaved and return home saved. What A Difference A Day Makes.

The late Sisters' Betty Williams and Estelle Williams helped me and others prayed and tarried (wait) with the students until they received the Holy Ghost. Sister Betty Williams taught me how to love every one of the students. She had a passion for their souls to be saved and her and her sisters Estelle and Janice were some of the greatest prayer warriors that taught me about Spiritual Warfare.

Betty was the first saint to invite me to their home for dinner. All these years I thought it was the fried chicken, chitterlings, collard greens, macaroni and cheese…that caused me to fall asleep on their sofa. But it was The Unshakeable Family Bond of Love for God and the peace that I was yoked to that day. I thank God for the gift of friendship for thirty-five years with Betty. She could always see God in every crisis. Janice is still healing, yet strong as ever, and we are still friends today. Many seasonal friends have come and gone, but I thank God for Warrior Women like Betty Williams and Janice Brown. Everyone needs a sister like Janice was to Betty. Remember, God gives friends described in Proverbs 17:17 "A friend loveth at all times; and a brother is born for adversity."

During summer vacations, I was able to minister in various cities. Within a year, the Lord blessed me to receive my ministerial license. It was also during this summer that the Lord instructed me to write this book. "A Book? Yes, Lord, whatever you say, I'll do it." The Lord taught me to hold my head up and not look back. Each relationship after those first years at Calvary were healthier ones. I felt free and began to feel whole. The brokenness, rather than anger and depression, was a stepping stone to wholeness.

Wholeness requires brokenness. It's not until I was broken that I could hear the Lord clearly and willingly surrendered my will. I understood that I no longer belonged to myself and life does not go my way, but the Lord's way, His will and His plan for me are the things that matter. His ways and thoughts are high above ours as high as the Heaven is from the earth. So what makes me think that He has to do it my way?

Remember, the fifth step is to RENEW my mind. I chose to think differently. I thanked God for using my pain to make me more dependent on Him. The more I depended on Him and His Word, the less I depended on people. My transformation was amazing. I was learning to change my mind to change my life and make permanent healthy changes. "You change your beliefs and you'll change your thoughts. Change your thoughts and you'll change your habits. Change your habits and your life opens to unlimited possibilities." Gail Lynne Goodwin.

Codependency is rooted in immaturity and must be changed by our thinking. Leave your childhood thinking and your dependent thinking that anyone is your all-in-all. Examine your patterns of thinking. Don't believe that pleasing people is always Christ like. Don't think that you should always say yes when you believe in your gut you should say no. Confess that you are trying to be God in the life of another person. Don't fear losing the love of others when you allow them to suffer the consequences of their negative actions. Realize you cannot make a person be dependable or responsible. Hebrews 6:1, "Let us go on to maturity...."

He created the Heavens and the Earth and knew me before I knew myself. He created me in His image and likeness. I was learning how to appropriate my identity in Christ Jesus. I can be set free because Christ lives in me. I can change my dependency on people through the power of Christ that lives in me. I can do everything through Him who gives me strength.

Many restored and transformed believers helped motivate me to dedicate my life to teaching, ministering, counseling and writing about mental health issues. Jesus is the Answer. Secular counseling helped. The medical profession was good. My families and friends love was invigorating, but, moving to Youngstown taught Shawnie and I more lessons on transformation that heals emotional wounds and makes us whole. We were learning about becoming partakers of the divine nature of Christ through His precious promises.

On two occasions I wanted to return to Michigan because I was unemployed and received an excellent job offer back home. When I asked Pastor, "Is this the will of the Lord, he said, No." I refused to take No for an answer, so I sent Elder A. Glenn Brady, now Bishop Brady, to explain the details, no money, no income, my daughter's in college, etc. The answer was still No. My friends were livid and felt that I was brainwashed by listening to a man. But, I knew that God gave him great revelations, discernment, visions, dreams etc. I heard the voice of God that day and said No!

If we'd moved back to Michigan, it would have been one of the greatest mistakes ever and interrupted God's perfect will for many lives. Within a month their facility was shut down and they moved out of state. God showed me not many days hence, that we would see the reality of His promises, and the unlimited possibilities open unto us. I was learning to celebrate the love that God has for me. God's promise to me was in Psalms 147:3, "He healeth the broken in heart and bindeth up their wounds." The Promises of God Makes The Difference.

CHAPTER 6
BELIEVE THE PROMISES OF GOD MAKES THE DIFFERENCE

We have been postured into an opportunity to become partakers of His divine nature. What a blessing. My daughter's grades began to miraculously improve. She received additional support during elementary school, because of difficulties at home. But, upon experiencing the love, compassion, care and concern from the entire Calvary staff, her grades improved to 3.0's. Another promise of God manifested! Remember he healeth the broken in heart and bindeth up our wounds.

Shawnie was supposed to visit my brother, Rex, in Florida for her summer vacation, but once again by divine leading, she was directed to visit her dad and his new wife, Linda (a kind stepmother) and little brother, fun-loving, Benny III, in Detroit, Micigan. Benny was only three years old and Shawnie was sixteen years old. Shawnie spent the day with her dad and he told her, "I want you to listen to your mom. She is a good and smart woman. I want you to graduate from high school and get a good education like your mother, you hear me?

Annoyed she replied, "Yeah, Dad" because he had been drinking. Linda, his wife, and Shawnie literally begged Benny to attend the wedding reception with them at Belle Isle Park.

He hesitated and said, "Yeah" then changed his mind and said, "You all go on. I'm staying home."

They left the house at mid-afternoon and when they returned six hours later, the lights were still off, the door still open and immediately Linda and Shawnie sensed trouble. They ran for help and one of the neighbors, a young man ran up the stairs with Shawnie right behind him. He kicked the door open and cursed.

Then he turned to Shawnie and yelled, "Go, back downstairs and call the police!"

Shawnie screamed, "No, Daddy, Daddy, Daddy" as he laid slumped over the toilet half dressed, with a needle in his body, and blood dripping from his mouth. The rescue team tried to revive him.

Then they covered him up with a white sheet and said, "He's dead!"

On Sunday, August 24, 1986, when the phone rang at 5:30 in the morning, I was still numb from sleep. I heard Shawnie say, "Mama, we found Daddy dead! He died from a drug overdose! I found him in the bathroom. Oh, Mama, he had a needle stuck in his body. He was already dead."

I immediately remembered the voice of the Lord that spoke to me eight years ago, and forewarned me of his death. After his death, Shawnie entered her senior year very depressed. The Lord performed a miracle, healing Shawnie's emotions, and delivering her from major depression. He healeth the broken in heart and bindeth up their wounds.

I was shocked, but the Lord kept me calm, even though I cried. I was angry and remember stating, "You broke your promise, and you couldn't even be here for her graduation. You always left me alone to raise Shawnie." I canceled his small term insurance policy in June, thinking Benny will probably live longer than me.

But, the Lord worked a miracle! I remembered an evangelist who stuttered while she ministered in Ypsilanti for our Women's Day, with a similar situation. She told us how she prayed and asked the Lord to honor the lapsed policy after she stayed with her abusive husband, out of obedience. God reminded me that He spoke to me years before Benny died through this woman who stuttered as she preached and that I would experience the same miracle. I prayed the same prayer, and the company did honor my lapsed policy as well. I used the money to pay off all our debts. Shawnie became eligible for a portion of his Social Security benefits, which was also divided between his wife and son.

God began to miraculously multiply our resources. On the day of the second hearing for my Social Security Disability, the judge shook his head in dismay. "You mean that you lived through all of this abuse and illness, and now you are able to work and maintain a household! Do you mean the other judge heard your case, and all of these details, and ruled against you! It is evident that you suffered from an emotional breakdown if you felt that a drug-addicted husband could care for your daughter better than you."

The Vocational Rehabilitation Counselor also stated that there was no way to maintain a job during my cyclical chemical imbalance crisis. Today, they label it Bi-polar II, or manic-depressive. I was confident and full of energy, then depleted, fatigued and insecure. I could swing high, then I could swing low, and vacillate often within two weeks monthly.

He yelled, "Previous decision overruled. I rule in favor of the applicant. Case Closed." God did it!

After a seven year battle, we won. I was able to use the retroactive disability lump sum for a closed period of three years to make the down payment on a house we'd always wanted. My attorney was an eye-witness to what the Lord can do in impossible situations.

Promise after promise continued to be fulfilled in our lives. Shawnie graduated from high school and entered Youngstown State University. Her advisor stated, "Based on her previous academic difficulties caused by emotional problems in the home, I feel she will only remain in college one year."

Based on all of the records and her profile as a child of a drug addict, it seemed it might be challenging for her to receive a college degree.

I remember speaking to a friend and colleague one day, who happened to be her second grade teacher.

He said, "Cheryl, when you get yourself together, Shawnie will be able to perform better and won't be depressed. At five years old, she is suffering from depression like you are." Shawnie had attended four different kindergartens in four states because of our moves from Ann Arbor to Detroit to Killeen, Texas, and back to Ypsilanti, Michigan. Those moves greatly affected her because she left Ann Arbor without processing the death of her favorite, 24 year old kindergarten teacher and role model who was killed in a car accident. At five years old, she also was grieving her separation from her father once again. Our circumstances and her grief strained our relationship. Now I know young children need counseling in order to process their emotions from their traumas.

Shawnie and I understood why the college advisor felt the way she did. But, the Lord made both of us a promise that if we moved in His will, and left Ypsilanti, and came to Youngstown, He would make up the difference. He did, and worked miracle after miracle in the process.

She continued to struggle to learn basic study skills as a college student, however, we put God first in prayer, fasting and meditating upon biblical principles to restore her worth and image in God. That time allowed me a great opportunity to demonstrate new parenting skills. I learned that it was never too late to be a godly parent, even if my child was nineteen before I finally learned how. We saw another promise answered. He restored my relationship with my daughter. My daughter graduated from Youngstown State University with her Bachelor's Degree in Psychology, debt free. We would receive grants and unsolicited scholarships and it was nobody but God who provided. He deserves the credit and the glory. With man this would be impossible, but with God all things are possible.

At the end of my fifth year of teaching school, I heard the Lord speak again, saying I was to leave the academy. I refused to resign and was fired. The School Board voted against my request to remain employed. Overnight, I found myself without a job. Fear took hold, but the Lord told me it was time for a new assignment and I knew that my assignment ended, but I couldn't resign so God simply released me.

Unemployment was a new experience in Canaan Land. The Lord used the saints to provide all of our needs. Psalms 23:1 The Lord is my shepherd, I shall not want. One friend said, "The Lord told me to pay your mortgage and all utilities until you are employed." The friend kept his promise, just as the Lord keeps His. He paid those bills for seven months. Other friends gave us groceries.

Community agencies once again became involved in a plan for my career change. They assisted in providing clothes and other needs. The showers of blessings continued for months.

Finally, an ad appeared in the local newspaper which provided an opportunity to work part-time in an interesting and challenging area, counseling and assisting AIDS clients at the very agency the Lord told me I would work months ago.

Another miracle! Someone else was hired after I'd been interviewed, and almost guaranteed the job. Disappointed, I told my friend, The Lord assured me for months that I would be employed at this agency.

One friend said, "I don't care who they hired, God said the job is yours and they will have to leave that job." Within one month, I received a call for a second interview and was hired. The employee suddenly quit within the month and accepted a job at another agency.

Their grant was tailored made for me because it stipulated that the qualifications for the position had to be a codependent, a family member of someone who chemically dependent/addicted. Look at God preparing me in the 70's, 80's for a ministry twenty years later in the late 80's and early 90's. While employed as an AIDS/HIV Counselor, and eventually, Case Manager, the culmination of all my spiritual and secular education, experiences, revelations, and holistic healing, maximized itself in this position. The diversity of requiring record keeping and communication, utilized my business education skills.

Networking with other institutions and professional contacts further developed my personality and demanded assertive skills. Public speaking and group presentations within the community reinforced the teaching and preaching skills I'd learned at Calvary. The outreach and counseling to the clients and their families, a ministry of compassion and encouragement, was most rewarding. I felt alive, and for the first time understood why it was necessary for me to live with a heroin addict for many years.

That experience qualified me to be sensitive and knowledgeable to the wants, needs, and concerns of the chemically dependent and their families. The clients targeted were those who were high-risk drug users. It enabled me to be sensitive to the multiple losses of physical and emotional health, loss of income, isolation and rejection in relationships they incurred when they received HIV positive tests results. I gave them genuine, unconditional love and provided community resources. I was able to give back to the community the support that was given to Shawnie and me years ago. I never forgot God's grace, love and kindness and I learned how important it is to pass it on.

As a delivered, former, healed, restored and transforming, co-dependent, I understood the spirit of addiction, and its effect. At agency group presentations, my director, supervisor, and co-workers, as well as the recipients, commented on my effective witness for the Lord Jesus Christ. One co-worker said my testimony had him in tears.

Frequent travel, training, and workshops continued to prepare me for dealing effectively with the clients. One of the last presentations made at a local hospital to doctors, nurses, social workers, and other helping medical professionals was most rewarding. The doctors admitted their lack of sensitivity to the client's plight, and were more willing to be less clinical, and more sensitive. That, for me, was a great milestone.

My other supervisor, from another city, was present. In two months she wanted me to speak at the State Case Manager's Update meeting in Columbus, and present the same seminar to enlighten other Case Managers of Community Networking Strategy that works so well for us. I was excited that God was doing miracles in healing my spirit, soul and body by providing me with strength to perform beyond my ability. Because of the heavy caseload, I was also told that one, and possibly two part-time case managers would be hired, and I'd be their supervisor. What a blessing! I had more help to accomplish the needs of the people, with a pure, sincere and honest motive.

The caseload increased and several of the clients were very pleased with their services. Celebrating my first anniversary on the job, I couldn't think of a better way than to celebrate with a new position and raise. Then suddenly without notice or warning, the pivotal day came, seemingly to defeat me, once again.

My supervisor came to my house on Friday, February 1, 1990 while I was working at home on a special assignment. She stated, "The director wants you to come to work today at 1:00 p.m. for a special meeting." I stated, "I called in this morning stating my house was burglarized and the back door is still not secured, may I come in on Monday?" She stated, "I'm not sure I'll have to call you back." While waiting on the call, in the pit of my stomach I felt sick. Something is wrong, I discerned a demonic presence, so I called a covenant prayer partner and asked her to pray. She said, I'm off work today. I'll go with you."

Once I received the call that the meeting was mandatory, I left the house unsecured, but trusted the angels and the blood of Jesus to keep it protected and arrived at the job site.

The director angrily stated, while my supervisor and assistant director were sitting staring at me with dismay: "We are terminating you because you were evangelizing on the job. One of the clients stated that you closed his case because he no longer continued to go to church with you. He's threatened to sue this agency and we can't have that. You also failed to pass out condoms and needles to your clients during your visitations. You have the option of quitting or being fired. We want you to turn in your key and the special project you've been working on at home. Only then will we release your check. We don't want you to report for work on Monday at YSU for the Aids Quilt Program."

In total shock, I looked in disbelief at each one of them and with composure and dignity responded, "I see you've already drawn your conclusion and made a determination without the courtesy of asking me what happened. I was told to close his case by both supervisors because this client failed to receive treatment for his cocaine addiction. They stated he was also manipulating the system. I just want to ask one question, "How could you take the word of a drug addict, a diagnosed paranoid schizophrenic, a habitual liar and ex-convict against my reputation?" When you told me we could pray for clients because this job was a ministry, I only prayed for people if they asked for prayer.

When you told me I could no longer pray for people even upon request, I no longer prayed openly for anyone else. The clients received their needles and condoms from the outreach workers who accompanied me. This client asked to attend Mt. Calvary because his sister in New York always told him for years, "The Lord is the only one who can help you now." He asked if I could take him and I told him no, but told him how to pursue it himself. He even manipulated the church for a while.

Once his case was closed, he told me he'd get even with me. He threatened me and I believe he's the one who broke into my house last night while we were at church. Furthermore, it is not my choice to terminate this employment, it's yours, but I will make the final decision when I return with your key."

As I walked, my legs could barely make it to the front door where my friend was waiting.

When I saw her, I was still in shock, I said, "They fired me! They said I was evangelizing on the job, I can't believe this." As we began to drive and cry, we returned with the key. I wiped my eyes, entered in and said to my supervisor,

"There's the key, I refuse to quit."

She said, "You're fired!"

I'd just stopped by the church to get prayer and counsel, which helped calm me down. My flesh was too weak to fight.

The day I was terminated, it happened to be the evening of our church communion after five days of fasting and praying. I've just experienced another major heartbreak and what message does God send? "From Broken Pieces." It soothed my pain. God said, "Now do you believe that I want you to complete your book, Broken to Be Made

Whole?" My response, "Yes, Lord." I finally discerned the "open door." It's not just a cliché but so very true, when God slams one door in your life, He opens a greater and better door and opportunity for you to walk through."

Even though I knew this was God's will, in my flesh, I experienced great sadness and I began to file grievances for unemployment benefits. I knew it was time to finish my book! That job was another turning point of my life. Old feelings of inadequacy and depression returned, but this time spiritual warfare was necessary. I was able to fight those spirits of self-pity, insecurity, fear etc. off with dignity, and without destructive anger. Neither my worth nor esteem were based on of the job, but God's Word. I was still the same person, whether employed or unemployed, and I maintained the same assets.

The Word of the Lord came once again, assuring me that everything would be alright. Entering a difficult time in obtaining unemployment benefits, the Lord once again sent a word. I inquired in prayer if the reason I was not receiving benefits was because I deserved to be terminated without being aware of the reason. He woke me up at 1:00 a.m. and said, "Turn to the book of Job and keep reading until I tell you to stop. He stopped me at Job 2:3 … "without cause …" That is the promise that I stood on when we fought for unemployment benefits. The Lord said I was fired without just cause, and that I would win the unemployment case even though there were three denials against me.

It was the most unusual unemployment case the State of Ohio said they ever had. Normally, the examiner hears the case within 45-60 minutes, but my case took 2 days, four hours each day. The first day the Lord said, "Take 7 others with you as you go." I thought they would be witnesses but they were not admitted. Instead, they circled in the hallway, joined hands and prayed. While I was alone on the inside with my attorney and the agency staff, the most amazing thing happened. Every time they would ask questions designed to accuse me of being incompetent, co-workers and supervisors could never say I was incompetent. The attorney used the tactics and tried to intimidate me by summarizing that I was lower than the client that accused me and a liar, who used this job to minister. My attorney surmised that I was different from the other employees and that they used the client as an excuse to get rid of me.

The decision was reversed again and overruled when the referee declared that I was fired without just cause and I'd performed my duties properly. He also stated that they fired me because I was different, holy and they interpreted that as being stuck up and thinking that I was better than them. I simply lived a different lifestyle and never fit in. I received retroactive unemployment benefits. Another miracle, and victory!

The Lord instructed me on Sunday, after 6 a.m. prayer, to drive to Dunkin Donuts. I only had forty cents. He instructed me what to say and He'd do the rest. The clerk went in the back and boxed one dozen donuts and said, "Here! No charge!" I left with tears in my eyes as the Lord said, "In your obedience, this is symbolic of all your provisions that I will supply for you. No welfare. Trust me." God gave us relentless favor, divine protection and divine provisions.

One agency called me for an interview. They were impressed with my record, and sensitivity as an AIDS Case Manager, and said they would contact me when they received funding. They received the money at the same time a new mental health agency was established at our church. Second Chances Christian Counseling received a temporary grant. Elder Daniel Newman interviewed, and greatly encouraged me, claiming I would be a great asset and resource person to the staff. He hired me as a professional Christian Counselor, about three hours before the other agency offered me a job for a few months. Wow two job offers.

Eventually, the job ended at Second Chances and the Lord spoke out of Heaven until my daughter who couldn't understand why I couldn't stay employed heard the Rhema Words of life as Bishop Wagner paraphrased, I don't care if you apply for a job and submit your resume on gold or rose colored paper, you will not be hired or if they do hire you they will fire you or you will quit. You belong to God and He's your new employer." Despite the joblessness, the miracles continued. The Lord keeps those in perfect peace whose mind is stayed on Him, and trust in Him. I have seen Him perform too many miracles not to trust Him. After my last unemployment, I understood that He will always provide.

Several requests for teaching and preaching engagements were offered, affording me the opportunity to travel and minister in several states. Ministering to the singles in the mountains of Pennsylvania was most rewarding. The five seminars dealt with finances, esteem, "single and satisfied," inner healing, and single-parenting.

While teaching at this particular retreat, I came to the conclusion that I was saved, single, satisfied, and believed it.

My happiness no longer depended on other people, or having a man in my life. I had become a whole human being, not just a half, trying to find a whole!

True happiness meant finding the will of the Lord, and using my gift to serve His people. I finally realized Who I Am in God.

God gave me favor with the late Elder Alfred Coward as we appeared on television twice to fight domestic violence. Appearing on the front page of the local newspaper was giving God glory. Look at God, He turned our messes into messages. My greatest blessings were the lives that were saved, touched, healed, encouraged and transformed. The victories or defeats depended on how I perceived each situation. I used the anger constructively by seeking the Lord in prayer for direction. What's Next Lord?

Many clients are still alive and doing well in spite of the prognosis which gave some of them only six months to live. Aware that at least three have been healed from AIDS, and to know that it is possible, is rewarding.

In the meantime, I had the opportunity to teach a seminar on III John 2. "Beloved, I wish above all things that you would prosper and be in health, as your soul prospers. The seminar was entitled, Beautiful Ishahah (Woman). It enhanced the sense of the total worth of a woman's body, mind and spirit in the Lord. My entire purpose for life is to be a beautiful woman for the Lord, according to His requirements ... not others. He sees me through His eyes of love.

Realizing the love of God bridges the gap between the Me who I see, the Me who you want me to be, the Me who others think I should be, and the Me who I want to be. I finally decided just to be me. My inner and outer realities of life were finally in sync with God's Word. At last, I was a genuine person.

I learned to take the string of desires, drives, habits, and lusts, and turn them over to the Lord in prayer, which creates spiritual energy. The more obedient I was, the better I felt. There was no more guilt for being hypocritical. No more pain from inner cravings. I was able to master the human desires by remembering the discipline the Lord taught me on that eighteen day fast, coupled with reading the entire New Testament. When I had an urge to please my flesh, I'd fall on my knees and pray until the desire left. Then I'd search the Bible concerning that particular temptation, and speak to my mind by rehearsing several times. Just as the desire for junk foods and other foods that weren't healthy ceased, the desire and cravings for attention, pity and help stopped.

The original being that God created was the real me, and the purpose of being born-again was to become the real me which is on the inside, not the outside. All the property we need is in being in the will of the Lord, and doing what he has called us to do.

What a freeing, liberating experience! Prophetically God sees me as whole. I am a whole egg.

Prior to my last period of unemployment, an interesting relationship developed with my new friend, Luther. It began as he left a message with one of ushers for me to wait for him after the service one day.

Remembering him as the young man who made an open prayer request, "I want a wife", I laughed, because I was the only sister who openly confessed "I want a husband." That night, my friend said, "You want a husband, there he is." We laughed, but from that time on I observed his faithfulness to the Lord. I watched from a distance, for almost two years. On that particular evening, I became curious why he wanted to talk to me.

He said, "I want to work with you in the recovery ministry. I want to help one of the clients you are working with who I grew up with in the housing projects." She was pregnant, recovering from her addiction to cocaine and newly saved. I agreed, and we worked on the case together weekly, but had no other contact when we came together. The first time the client was admitted to rehabilitation out of town, we visited her together and he treated me to lunch. At that point, I realized he was very nice, but not for me.

Over the months, we became best friends and we discussed who we were interested in with one another. We prayed that the Lord would bless us with those people. However, one day the Lord chastened me and spoke, "I did not tell you to pray for that union, pray according to my will." That was truly the Lord. It is the way Pastor Wagner teaches us to pray for companionship; not for a specific person, but for the attributes of the type of mate we desire, and then allow the Lord to work. As a result, I never prayed out the will of the Lord again for Luther.

Luther liked several sisters, but he liked one in particular. Several sisters also liked him. Our friendship deepened through the months. He prayed with me during another miracle when I was again afflicted with larger tumors and small cysts. A possibility of cancer existed, but many of my church family prayed for healing. I received the first healing in my mouth where a dentist thought that there was a tumor. I believed the Lord for the abdominal healing also. Once again unemployed, I did not have the medical coverage for a major surgery, but the Lord spoke and said to proceed. The expenses were in excess of $10,000 this time, and once again the Lord provided and the expenses were covered.

Coming out of surgery I was blessed to learn there was no cancer. Luther took a vacation day every Monday for eight weeks and helped me around the house. We began to become covenant prayer partners, reading through the Bible for months and fasting together. As best friends, we shared secrets and he helped me study for my final exam in graduate school that summer.

After twelve months of ministry and friendship, the Lord began to make his intentions known to me through another friend. "This is your husband. He is too attentive to you just to be your friend. He honestly treats you better than some husbands treat their wives."

I laughed and told her, "He only likes me as a friend."

As I traveled to Michigan that June, I met Evangelist Peterson. Before she boarded the Greyhound Bus, I heard the Lord, "Take your Bible out of your purse and place it on your lap." In obedience, I did. When she saw the Bible, she asked, "Do you mind if I sit next to you?"

I said, "No, I don't mind." In the course of conversation, she began to prophesy, "You were the Black sheep of your family and have experienced a lot of pain in your life. You are unemployed and wonder how you are going to survive. You're even concerned about a certain man in your life. You have fought sickness. They even thought you might have cancer. In fact, your stomach is hurting right now. You have tears that are welled up, but when I pray for you, God will deliver you, and you will no longer worry about cancer. You are a blessed woman of God. You will marry before the end of the year, and when you set your wedding date, send me an invitation. I will come. You are going to be used in a great way in the city you are going to visit. And, you will receive financial blessings."

After she gave the prophecy she fell asleep as if she were dead. I nudged her, "Are you okay?" Startled, she opened her eyes for a moment, "Yes, baby, I'm okay."

I said, "Well, we're in Ypsilanti, my stop, God Bless You. I'll write soon."

True to the Word of the Lord, while visiting my former pastor, Elder Ross, in the hospital two days before he died, I met a woman in the hallway who knew Evangelist Helen Taylor. She complained about the arthritis in her hands and how she was unable to move them. We anointed them with blessed oil and prayed for her healing. Immediately she began to move them crying. "Oh, Lord, I'm healed! I have not been able to move my hands for a long time. I'm healed." God healed her.

Back in Youngstown, two weeks later, I had a new attitude. I was instructed by my mentor, Pastor Yvonne Hawkins-Bell and friend, Elder Gerald Morgan, not to spend as much time with Luther, but to continue to be used in ministry. I felt if he really wasn't interested in me, that he needed to go his way and I go mine because we were hindering one another from receiving our blessings.

But, every time we agreed to separate, something happened to draw us together again. He helped me pack to sell my home, because Shawnie was graduating from college. Being unemployed, and living from day to day at the hand of the Lord, I thought an apartment would better suit me. I could use the money from the sale of the house. It was a set-up, I never sold the house at that time. But God promised me a good husband and I trusted Him to choose my husband for me this time.

The promises of God enhanced my emotional intelligence and my ability to trust the right sources, unbeknown to me at the time. These promises began to heal my perception and belief system as I began to become a partaker of His divine nature and grew in grace.

Promise defined by Merriam-Webster is a declaration that one will do or refrain from doing something specified. A promise is a legally binding declaration that gives the person to whom it was made a right to expect or to claim the performance or forbearance of a specified act. There is a distinct difference between man made promises, which can be broken and the Promises of God that are never broken.

The Promises of God are defined as the declaration or assurance which God has given in His Word of bestowing blessings on His people. Such assurance is resting on perfect justice, power, benevolence and immutable veracity of God that cannot fail. II Peter 3:9 states, "The Lord is not slack concerning His promises." God's promises are divine. The promises of God reveal His particular and eternal purposes to which He is unchangeably committed and upon which believers can totally depend. These promises are, however, conditional upon obedience on the part of the believers and requires a "resolve" in your spirit. A resolve is to come to a definite or earnest decision about; determine to do something. To deal with, settle or solve a matter of uncertainty. Resolutions are plans for developing your character defects and transforming from who you are to who God created you to be, whole. You learn to resolve to live internally as opposed to externally.

The promises of God shine the light on problems and provide solutions. The promises of God provides HOPE during the process of change. II Corinthians 1:20, "For all the promises of God in Him are yea, and in Him Amen, unto the glory of God by us." What God promises to us is already done before the foundation of the world. When we desire the manifestation of the promises, we ascend into Heaven to Worship, Praise and Prayer and access what has been waiting for us. God already made the decision to bless us, so we're not waiting on God, but God is waiting to be gracious to us when we learn to operate in faith, timing and spiritual discernment.

God's promises requires love, obedience, faith and discernment. These promises are given not only to bless us and grant healings and miracles, but to cleanse us as we mature and develop. God prepares us to be empowered and to transcend life's adversities into testimonies for God's Glory. God's promises are conditional based upon obedience.

Unlimited possibilities were opened unto us. Open doors are recognizable when we arrive to them because the Bible states that we will see many adversaries or adversities. I didn't realize that these "open doors" followed the spiritual transformation.

Happiness and joy doesn't depend upon who you are or what you have; it depends solely upon what you think according to God's will. Spiritual discernment stresses accuracy, and is the ability to tell the difference between the truth and error. Discernment is a means for creating space for God's activity and promises in our lives, making ourselves available so that He can do for us what we can't do for ourselves.

My friend, Evangelist Ivy Caddell, called me one day and reminded me of the description of my husband. Even though I thought I had one description, she said that Luther fit the one that the Lord had given her years ago, while we lived in Ypsilanti. She told me, "Seek the Lord, take your special self to your special God, and ask Him to reveal His will one more time. I'm going to pray with you concerning your wedding date. It will be this year, even though it doesn't seem like it is coming to pass." I finally realized that Luther would be my spouse.

The pastor always said, "If the Lord made you a promise, go back and read it. Keep it alive in your mind." Reading my diary, I saw where the Lord told me in January that Luther was to be my husband. But due to many circumstances, I'd forgotten, or stopped believing.

Luther took seven months to realize that I was to be his wife, but during that entire time, I never tried to convince, persuade, or help him make a decision. I waited while he attempted to date others. God had already completed the work.

In the meantime, several prophecies and confirmations came forth stating I would be married by the end of 1991. In June, Luther was still stating, we're just friends. Somewhat confused and frustrated, I sought the Lord again.

He said, "When you stop listening to what Luther says, and listen to Me, I'll bless you. What is the name of the Sunday School lesson you are teaching?"

I replied, "God against the Odds."

He said, "Believe me."

My response, "Yes, Lord!"

At that point, my faith reached an all-time high. The Lord was working out another promise. At the end of the fourth consecutive week of wearing white apparel, Luther proposed, on July 24, 1991. He immediately purchased my engagement ring, a butterfly ring, on July 27, 1991. Luther knew nothing about the significance of a butterfly to me, but I cherished the butterfly engagement ring, realizing our union was the perfect will of the Lord.

Preparation for marriage had already begun in our friendship as we'd read books on Walking in Love, viewed video tapes on successful marriages, and attended Sunday Academy, and other seminars on marriage.

Our parents, and both families liked our decision, and were happy. We listed our goals and commitments to one another. This time it was not an emotional, irrational decision based on feelings of lust, but based on true love. I finally learned how to make a healthy decision regarding my mate.

Luther was different than any man I ever spent quality time with. He was kind, considerate, gentle, giving, firm, stable, physically built, slightly taller than me, about same complexion just a bit lighter, and attractive to me. He was raised by his mother and sister, and was extremely loving and attentive to them. He was the right person sent by the Lord God Himself, and worthy of my love. He was truly committed to the Lord first, me second, Shawnie third, and his family, ministry fourth.

True love is not a feeling, but a commitment, something that was always lacking in my former relationships. As long as I had a fear that I would never marry a good man, and remained an emotional cripple, waiting for marriage to rescue me, I'd remain single. But, as soon as I used the time alone to personally develop in my spirit, soul, and body, and was whole, and began to give unconditionally to others, the Lord sent a godly man tailored made for me.

We attended premarital counseling, but our engagement wasn't official until three months later. Using wisdom, the pastor allows the couple time to reevaluate their decision, and discover one another.

We abstained from sex. Our lives were pure before the Lord, the pastor, family, and friends when we knelt at the altar for marriage. Such a great, clean feeling! God has granted us favor. God kept me abstinent for ten years from the time of my divorce from Benny until the night of mine and Luther's honeymoon. We are celebrating twenty-nine years today, as I'm inserting the final revisions on November 16, 2020. Thank You Jesus for the victory and knowing it is possible with Him.

Unable to afford a large wedding, we wanted an office wedding and a small reception at our home, but the Lord that I serve has always provided. The Lord used the saints. They encouraged us to have a small church wedding and donated money, time, and energy to enable us to marry at the church, and have a lovely reception.

Another miracle! The saints were such a blessing. The cost of the wedding to us was minimal, and the monetary gifts from our family and friends were unbelievable, 100 times more than we spent on the wedding. It's truly the marriage that is more important than the wedding day, unless you can truly afford a lavish wedding, then go for it. We were able to pay our tithes, go on a honeymoon, purchase three large items for our home, repair the floor, and still have a few dollars left over to save.

This is the revelatory promises that ushered us out of Michigan and into Ohio in Genesis 12:1-3, "Now the Lord had said unto Abram, get thee out of thy country, and from thy kindred, and from thy father's house, unto a land that I will show thee: And I will make of thee a great nation, and I will bless thee, and make thy name great; and thou shalt be a blessing: And I will bless them that bless thee, and curse him that curseth thee: and in thee shall all families of the earth be blessed. The Lord God reminded me of His promises to us as we crossed the state line when He whispered, "**I will bless you with a good husband, I will bless you in ministry, I will heal your broken hearts and bind your wounds. I will bless your seed and all of the family members that bless you. I will bless you financially.**"

It's The Process and Not the Promise alone that heals. Psalms 147:3, "He healeth the broken in heart and bindeth up their wounds."

"Every promise has a process and there is a prescribed way to accomplish the thought of God in your life and in your dream. It's important to know the process, how God moves in your life and agree with the process. The problems of yesterday must give way to the promise of your tomorrow. God keeps His promises because there is always a purpose for the promise to fulfill our healing, His perfect will, for us to live an abundant life. We are always living in God's purpose (The Promised Land) because we are here by His divine providence. There is always providence, purpose, a proceeding Word, a promise and a process with pain on purpose.

The purpose of the promise is found in II Corinthians7:1, "Having therefore these promises, dearly beloved, let us cleanse ourselves from all filthiness of the flesh and spirit, perfecting holiness in the fear of God." He sends His promise before the pain and then heals us in the pain.

Yes! Promise, after promise, after promise manifested in our lives. Some came immediately, others we missed, and yet others we had to wait in blood, sweat and tears. Just as important as my new name was my new attitude as a result of my renewed mind. I had years of insecurities, but the God of all grace was healing me and giving me a second chance.

It was exciting to experience the challenges of living in a blended family. "Luther, you love Shawnie just like she's your own daughter. And there is nobody like "Gran-gran" in Maya's life. Thank you for loving them. A family faces a problem directly and deals with it that day; pain is resolved by talking things out and coming to a resolution. Pain must be talked out and prayed through otherwise burying pain will only cause more problems. Psalms 32:3 states "When I kept silence my bones waxed old through my roaring all the day long." The roaring all day long indicated built up anger.

In blended families today, Shawnie could have perceived Luther as an intruder, however, he did take the time to do what so many other potential stepparents need to do, and that is intentionally build relationships with the children.

It takes time for the adult children and a step-parent to blend. In premarital counseling, issues of blended families are addressed and worked through. Blended families need goals. God created marriage and the family as a ministry. The goal is to develop oneness between Luther, the husband and me, his wife. The unity of Luther and I, the spouses, had to be unquestionably strong in order to build a bond with the children and present a stable home. We did not allow Shawnie nor Maya to become manipulative and destructive to our relationship. Pastor advised me on how to be a newlywed, a mother to an adult daughter and a new grandmother.

God used Luther for supernatural intervention and restoration in maturing me to oneness and wholeness. His character of integrity, consistency, commitment, generosity, honesty, selflessness, sacrificing, and unconditional love manifests itself and taught me how to love. It is mysterious because oneness includes spiritual oneness, sexual oneness, and emotional oneness.

To maintain this oneness, we began our marriage by celebrating our monthly anniversary. Every 16th of the month we'd alternate and choose a variety of ways to celebrate. Then as we could afford it, we began weekly date nights alone to discuss issues, share God's word, and pray together. Annually, Luther, on our yearly anniversary in our hotel room, Luther would present our accomplished goals, financial status and short and long term goals in elaborate notebooks with pages upon pages of colorful facts and statistics.

Together we'd discuss our life for the future.

Were there challenges? Yes! Were there sacrifices? Yes. In blended families, someone inevitably will enter the marriage with unresolved conflicts and unhealed internal wounds where children sometimes still have hope that Mom and Dad will get back together. Shawnie's Dad was deceased, however, she still had the memories of her dad and memories of painful and abusive incidents. There were some good memories to reflect on with him, but Shawnie shared more memories recently that had a positive and profound effect on her. We loved our Bass-Guster family and our in-laws'/in-love, loved us. God used them and others as expressions of His divine love.

After testing Luther's love for her and observing his fairness, integrity and consistency, her fear of abandonment and being left out was resolved. A person who has been rejected and deserted may be so insecure that each absence from home of the new spouse could be a time of uncertainty until the person physically is present again. I remember often being so happy and yet anxious that something would happen to Luther. Now that I am enjoying a healthy marriage, God broke that spirit of fear.

We are all products of past life experiences, both good and bad. Luther needed insight on the characteristics of anxiety and depressive behaviors which caused him to be empowered rather than feel guilty that he couldn't "fix" our challenges. Women, wives simply desire our husbands to listen and be an emotional support, but by their very nature, Luther desired to get straight to the problem and provide an immediate solution.

God began to release Shawnie and me from the anxiety of domestic violence and give us joy, laughter and renewed our trust in relationships. We played games, tennis, bowled, traveled together and experienced the challenges of healing together. God gave Shawnie an article that she's written entitled, "Hurt to Heal." We had to be in the same home to experience it together. When anxiety was great within me or Shawnie, and her anger from unmet needs as a child were directed at me, Luther was the intercessor who had divine wisdom and imparted the principles of forgiveness in me when I was the target of her anger.

Shawnie and Maya lived with us for almost two years and blessed us to learn great lessons on unconditional love. I was able to prophesy to Shawnie regarding her future.

"God says, Community Corrections Agency is where you will be employed, and how do I know? Because the same God that shared with me it was time to leave Calvary Christian Academy and work at the Chemical Dependency Agency is speaking to me now. Our experiences with your Dad as co-dependents and victims of domestic violence are not in vain. God will take the same comfort He gave us and use us to comfort others at your new job. Of course, she went to Detroit, Michigan and all over the will of God until He slammed every door in her face and again, an "open door" was provided at Community Corrections. At the end of the fifth year, you will meet your husband at the job."

Luther and I keep her encouraged and helped her to remain on a very challenging job for eight years. The favor of the Lord was upon her and after eight years she was able to resign and her husband, David, supported her vision to open her home daycare which was her heart's desire. For a period of time she cared and nurtured children who are raised by single parents, much like the home daycares she was in, while I worked as a single parent.

"Luther, I love you so much, you had to make a great transition quickly on how to be a husband, father and grandfather, with all women in the house quickly."

One of the most challenging promises manifested twelve years after our marriage. God said, "I want you to look for a new home." Shawnie purchased our home, and we moved into an apartment believing it'd only be a few months until we found a home. A few months turned into years, years and years and the apartment began to close in on me after seven years.

The promises of God are yea and amen, but the process is the challenge. One Bible class God sent an encouraging word through our pastor: "I just walked in your house. Just now. It's a new house! You're sitting at the table with a manuscript. God's getting ready to use that book. Someone is at the table with you in that house, and is going to open a door that has never been opened before. God said, "Get quiet and get still and He said write only as I lead you. Do not write in the regular manner you have been writing books. Put the pen down and do not be alarmed if I don't show up for seven weeks. Stay still but when I come, I will finish it. By the name of the Lord Jesus Christ I have given unto you power and wealth for the Kingdom sake. You are part of the revelatory message of the Name of Jesus for the end time. Prepare for the greatest move of God and thank me that I have chosen you, The Lord said so." N.L. Wagner

I fell out of my seat unto the floor and wept and wept and wept for seemingly hours, but it was near the end of Bible class, so I believe it was only fifteen minutes or so. "

Even though the prophetic promise was spoken seven years after our marriage, it was not fulfilled until our twelfth year regarding the new home.

Once again divinely inspired, Sis. Beverly Smith, who had the patience of Job for seven years as she showed us over 77 houses, left a message on the answering machine and said, "Cheryl, I found your house. It's on the West side, a three year old home, two story with three bedrooms, a deck, a fireplace, living room, dining room, full basement, one and a half bathrooms, and a large master bedroom. It has a two and a half car garage, a fence and more."

After looking at 77 houses and still counting, I'd just decided to remodel the apartment and save more money then look a few more years from now. However, God taught me a valuable lesson. It was no longer the season nor the time to save, but sow a seed (give money to others) for the benefit of others and the seeds would multiply. We were learning to make room for the promise by sowing seeds to other causes.

Luther was eager to see the home, I called Beverly and said, "Beverly, I'm tired, it's not me that wants to see the home, but Luther. This is the same street I asked Luther to look at for over three years while the development was being built and each time he'd say, no, these homes are too small, I want a huge family room. So I don't know what makes him think they've gotten any larger, but he wants to see it."

On September 25, 2002, Elder Condridge Smith, Beverly Smith, Luther and I were scheduled to see the home at 2:30 p.m., immediately after morning service. While I was seated in the pulpit, we'd just given in an offering and Pastor spins around looks at me and says that God said, take another offering and when you seed, name your seed. He then walks away, spins back around and says Cheryl, God said when you give this seed, and it will become a down payment for your new home. The seed was a great sacrifice for us, at that time. The four of us looked at Pastor in amazement. He had no idea we were still looking at houses. I'd recently been in the office and shared with him that God revealed to me the day I'd missed our house. It wasn't that God hadn't fulfilled His promise, but I missed the process totally, listening to someone else and now I'm tired.

Yet, immediately, without hesitation for dinner or any other stops, the Smiths and Fosters rushed to the West Side, and lo and behold, as we walked in the door of this beautiful home, it had almost everything we'd asked for except the large family room. It was beautifully painted and decorated and we knew that this was our home. It was just for the two of us. However, the asking price was too steep for us.

While in the midst of the process of countering our lower bid on the house, I showed it to someone, and she said, "Girl, you better forget countering for a couple of thousand dollars and tell them to secure this deal. I said, "Let me call Luther and see what he says, then

I'll call Beverly." She said, "Call Luther later, call the realtor and explain to Luther later. Sure enough, there was a back-up bid that came in waiting for us to make a decision. The house was only on the market four days and already someone walked in right behind us and wanted to purchase it as well. But God highly favored us. Luther was fearful of the increased expenses which was four times greater than the apartment, but Pastor gave Luther a direct word during our next service. We signed the contract for the home and moved in on December 4, 2002.

The sixth step is a resolve, a bull dogged tenacity in your spirit. A resolute, absolute conviction in your spirit, mind, soul and body, that this is God and His absolute will. To resolve means to make a decision about something. It's also a definite or earnest decision about; a determination to do something. Promises require an undeniable belief, trust and confidence that God is a promise keeper. Hebrews 11:6, "But without faith it is impossible to please him: for he that cometh to God must believe that he is God, and that he is a rewarder of them that diligently seek him." Promises require faith, which is the assurance, hope, and conviction of the unseen.

Luther resolved in his heart to purchase our home and God miraculously blessed and with no down payment. God did it. Life was wonderful. "I can't wait to see what else is going to happen next, and hear the direction for the new-year at our New Year's Eve service. With a husband, new family, and a progressive ministry, what else did God have planned for us? The New Year's Eve message: This Is the Day I Changed, challenged me by the first introductory words. The power to change lies in your ability to direct and manage your emotions."

We traveled abroad to England, the Bahamas and nationwide as witnesses, ministering our story, giving God glory and making the books available as tools. Life was wonderful, the marriage was wonderful. We also taught weekend marriage retreats in the Pennsylvania area, and helped those seeking healing and salvation. God Did It. I'm not trying to be modest or humble, honestly, to this day I still don't know how God used us. It's His Amazing Grace because I know that we are the foolish things of this world that God used to awaken others to their ministry call. I still laugh today after I've heard many people say, "If God can use her, I know He can use me." or "I know that was God because it sure wasn't her." What they saw was the hand and favor of God on our lives and they beheld His Glory and was inspired to move into their ministries by God using very unassuming looking vessels to motivate them.

Yes, God blessed Luther and I with a very good marriage, but moved us to a good, godly marriage as we learned to love one another's strengths and weaknesses. It wasn't always easy. It took years to learn to love without throwing in the towel. God blessed us for over twenty-nine years and counting, to be "living testimonies" of His restorative powers by putting the broken pieces of our lives back together again as we became one. Yes, I had the emotional problems with anxiety and depression which eventually caused chronic health issues. Luther had broken pieces laying around also, as wonderful as he is. His deafness from birth in one ear caused some real communication problems in our marriage that we learned to overcome.

The Biblical principles and life-skills we learned catapulted us to a place in ministry far beyond our expectations, enabling Luther and I to travel to several states and abroad. Every promise is tested. Marriage is being interdependent upon one another for love after we receive all of our emotional needs met by God by living in our purpose.

He is a jealous God, even of the mate He gave you. I unconsciously replaced Him with the love of my husband and serving others. The busyness left me little time to practice the lessons I learned and even less time to continue my intimate relationship with God. Just like the beautician who doesn't have time to do her own hair, the mechanic who doesn't have time to repair his family's cars and the preachers who have time to save everybody except themselves. I was not yet whole, but aware that I was changing as God exposed layers of lies that resided within me.

Everything I depended on was outside of me. God's decisive timing knocked all the crutches out from under me, left me suspended in mid-air to listen to the Creator rather than the created. My life sources were cut out as Luther began his own menopause (andropause) and spent more time with his ailing Mom, and I my ailing Dad. My friends labeled me anointed, but needy and some withdrew their love and support and some friends died. What a shock! I was like Jacob where the Bible states, "And Jacob was left alone and he wrestled with God and begged Him not to leave him until He changed him." I thought Jacob was left alone for one year, but I was left alone for over twelve years, basically in silence compared to my previous social interactions.

The huge love deficits, and looking for someone other than God where I was bent, or bowed over was challenged. It was now time for me to stop being bent out of shape by horizontal, outside relationships and straighten up into my vertical relationship with God. Unknowingly idolizing my spouse, while ill, I went through a twelve year detoxification from anything in my system that came before God, friends, exercise, money, food, television, ministry, business ventures, counseling, spouse and family.

Remember anything in our lives that hasn't been transformed will be transferred and live in our history. Well, I began reverting back to some of my old self in my forties, then fifties. Many habits, behaviors and hurts I'd overcome twenty, thirty years ago. These old ways and mindsets reoccurred and it wasn't long before… I crashed, smashed, and broke into smithereens, again! Life became a continuous process of straightening up, releasing sin behavior patterns and staying in a vertical relationship with God. There I entered seemingly endless times of brokenness.

But in retrospect it was all part of the restorative and transforming process.

What a mid-life crisis and predicament to be in. Is it possible that some of us have lived in the illusion of happiness, and wholeness, only to discover that we are still lacking and missing some pieces?" Menopause, the mid-life crisis was the best of times and the worst of times. One of the transitional passages of life that can stop you dead in your tracks if there were any developmental tasks that you were deficient in, underdeveloped or ignorant of. Every seven years, life comes back to demand that you revisit and transform under developed areas. If you bypassed any areas in your life and just survived, you have a golden opportunity to get it right during these intervals of life so you will thrive.

I celebrate the love that God has given me as I'm broken, but for the last time.

SECTION FOUR
WHOLENESS

CHAPTER 7
BROKEN, BUT FOR THE LAST TIME

On September 2003, I was awakened at midnight and went into the guest bedroom as I heard God begin to share with me that I would be dead on arrival. My life changed forever from that day to the present. Not fully understanding, I shrugged it off as a message that maybe he was developing in my spirit. Only to hear God remind me one month later on that faithful day of October l8, 2003,

"Won't you please stay close to me today. Sit in my presence. Draw nigh unto me and I will draw nigh unto you." After three hours from 5:00 a.m. to 8:00 a.m. I heard Him say, "Go to the church to the intercessors prayer, and stay until I breathe on you." After about 10 minutes I felt this strong, cool, refreshing breath of God on me, and truthfully I didn't want to leave, but I followed his directives. Later that day I was challenged with my right leg, which had become numb and swollen in the back of the knee. I heard God instruct me to elevate my leg.

Eventually Luther said, "Why don't you call Doctor Jessie, my Friend, who is a nurse. I was advised to check out what we thought may have been an insect bite only to be whisked in an ambulance to St. Elizabeth's Hospital, which is approximately 10 miles from the Beeghly Emergency Center. In shock, I was admitted due to a d.v.t. (deep vein thrombosis) blood clot of the leg.

If I'd not discerned that sweet familiar voice, and failed to heed the warning from the Lord God Almighty to curtail and reduce my activity, I would have been dead on arrival at the hospital. The x-ray technologist stated, "This blood clot was hidden deep in your veins, I almost didn't see it."

Never having this illness before, I believed my hospital stay would be brief so that I would be able to travel to Toronto, Canada where I was to minister for Sis. Karen Bryan at a Women's Retreat. Each day I was pretty upbeat until I was convinced by loved ones and the hospital staff that this was a life threatening, potentially fatal illness. Even though I was receiving medications, they do not dissolve the clot, but my body must fight for me to dissolve the clot through rest, quiet and stillness. If the blood clot moved before the body dissolves it, the clot could travel to the lungs and I'd had a pulmonary embolism, or the heart and I'd suffer a fatal heart attack, or the brain, which would cause a stroke.

GOD is my healer. He kept and delivered me from this life-threatening experience. Following this season of deliverance, I was immediately catapulted into a season of solitude, over a twelve year period of time where I began to receive one stress related diagnosis after another. I received sixteen diagnosis and was taking over twenty-two pills daily, but God was still my healer.

I entered a season of seemingly endless times of brokenness. After the blood clot I was diagnosed with: Hashimoto's Thyroid disease, Bi-polar II Depression, Panic Attacks, Post-Traumatic Stress Disorder, Pre-Diabetes, Adult Attention Deficit, Brain Tumor, Irritable Bowel Syndrome-Chronic Constipation, Poor Immune System, Frozen Left, then Right shoulder, Neuropathy, Neural Stenosis, Fibromyalgia, Acid Reflux, Allergies, Sinus infections and Non-Specific Dermatitis. You name it, I was afflicted literally from head to toe. Psalms 34:19, Many are the afflictions of the righteous, but the Lord shall deliver them from them all."

The late Dr. Henry Wright states, stress disorders or syndromes are a result of fear, anxiety, stress, guilt and shame. The enemy causes you to lose your peace by producing fearful thoughts in you that affect your central nervous system. You begin to feel brain fog, and experience a host of other symptoms among the most common stress disorders are fibromyalgia, chronic-fatigue syndrome, type 2 diabetes, hypertension, irritable bowel syndrome, ulcerative colitis, chronic insomnia, migraines, and acid reflux." You internalize what you are fearing and your limbic system responds to the fear and your hypothalamus senses you are not at peace. It causes miss-fired electrical and chemical signals to go out of the body and cause dis-ease of function in the endocrine system, the nervous system, the digestive system, or all of the above. The real solution is to align my spirit and soul with the Word of God, to meditate on the Word and walk until it becomes a part of your long-term memory, replacing the stress-filled lies of the enemy. Then peace---not fear and stress—will reign in your heart and your life.

Post-traumatic stress disorder is a result of trauma involving fear, anxiety, and stress. PTSD always enlarges the amygdala. The amygdala is part of the spirit-soul-body connection in the brain. It helps us process feelings and thoughts that come out of the cerebral cortex. The amygdala is the first receiver of highly charged negative thoughts that originate from a spirit of fear. If the amygdala swells, the frontal or prefrontal cortex's ability to rationalize or process functional thoughts is hindered. When the emotions override the thinking part of the brain everything comes blasting through, and can cause illnesses or a psychosis. When the amygdala is normal before a trauma whether it is war, rape, being a victim of a crime, death of a loved one, or these natural disasters, or Covid19 coronavirus pandemic, the individual is still able to process the thoughts, images, trauma and battle. But for someone who has an enlarged amygdala before they experience the above traumas, their brains will not allow their thoughts in their prefrontal and frontal cortex to process thoughts and come to a proper conclusion. God does golden repairs and He will send His Word and heal and make us whole.

God gave me the scriptures and the promise in St. Matthew 9:20-22, "And, behold, a woman, which was diseased with an issue of blood twelve years, came behind him, and touched the hem of His garment: For she said within herself, if I may but touch the hem of His garment I shall be made whole. But Jesus turned about, and when He saw her, He said, Daughter, be of good comfort thy faith hath made thee whole. And the woman was made whole from that hour." When she "touched" the hem of His garment with a certain sound at the deep dimension, at the delta level, according to Dr. Kevin K. Daniels, mental health wellness and healings can occur.

I was so broken like this woman with the issue of blood, until I was desperate enough to place a demand on God, to receive deliverance. God can heal children and adults who suffered from toxic stress as a result of ACE, Adverse Childhood Experiences, and deliver Christians from the spiritual roots of bondage attached to those experiences. I BELIEVE GOD.

Many asked the question, "How many times do you need to be broken?" or "I don't believe that it takes all of that." However, God rarely heals all the brokenness in a person's life at one time, just ask Apostle Paul. He was told, "My grace is sufficient for you", when he sought healing for the thorn in his flesh. I was truly broken all over again and again and again to be made whole, and God's grace has been sufficient. The late Deacon Joseph Levels stated, "It takes a life-time to make a saint."

Dr. Henry W. Wright states, "We live in a culture where everything is judged by performance. We don't make allowances for people's failures because there is a stigma that everything we do must be perfect. This state of affairs creates a lot of stress and anxiety in people's lives. When they internalize this stress, it starts to affect their soul and many bodily systems. The result is they may end up with a stress disorder."

During our ministerial training session, the late Bishop Norman L. Wagner taught us, "Within a church family, there will always exist the need for counseling. The complexity of life and living often places one in a maze with no exit sign for normality. It is at this point one seeks the advice of many and sometimes the counsel of the insight of God.

Though our counsel is based upon the teaching of the scriptures, we must understand that the maze is construction by the ways of erring, broken men; consequently, one must understand the maze." "Often men and women are destroyed by the lack of knowledge of how to move from the place of their brokenness, last hurt or last failure into a place of both victory, joy and wholeness. The scripture tells us that the people of God are destroyed for the lack of knowledge. Christians are very unique because they have gained spiritual knowledge and have closed their minds and become rigid and resistant to the emotional and physical needs.

Inasmuch as knowledge is accumulated and stored by the faculty of the brain, the emotional state of a man is often overbearing. Whenever this happens, a person short-circuits. In common terms, he blows a fuse or becomes stressed out.

Nowadays, when all the lights go out (or we are stressed out) on a particular floor of a home, it simply means that the overload has tripped the circuit. To revive the lights in the house again, one must go to the place of the tripped circuit and push or restore again."

Churches today play a crucial role in deliverance from the spiritual roots of stress disorders, the way to mental health wellness and wholeness. We have ignored the broken habits and broken patterns, or "the elephants in the rooms" in many of our homes and churches for too long. No matter how long we have been saved there are still areas in our lives that we serve Satan in whether we want to believe it or not. Until we humble ourselves and face our issues, we will remain underdeveloped and unaware of our infirmities.

BROKEN TO BE MADE WHOLE

St. John 5:6 When Jesus asks a question that depicted my lifetime struggle with generational iniquities and bondages rooted in the unloving spirit, anxiety, stress and fear for decades my answer was, "Yes!" This lame man who was stricken in his body for over thirty eight years became my object lesson. He was delivered, but, not developed and Jesus found him in the church and said "sin no more." Ecclesiastes 9:11b states, ".....but time and chance happeneth to them all. Jesus provides the opportunity for deliverance and development to each and every one of us to be made whole. When He visits you and ask this pertinent life changing question, Wilt thou be made whole? My answer was "Yes!" This passage depicted my lifetime for decades. Well, get ready to be broken to be made whole. God never breaks us unless He makes us. God never makes us unless He breaks us. We make the choice, God makes the change. God is responsible for our consequences of our choices and we are responsible for our choices in righteous or unrighteousness.

Understanding the positive attributes of brokenness is the steppingstone to an abundant life.

Broken, defined in Hebrew, "Shabar" means to be broken in pieces, to be torn violently or shattered, to sliver, to shatter, or to reduce to fragments; to fracture, ruptured; not properly functioning; out of order and splintered. It also means the mental anguish that comes from a devastating psychological blow. The implication is that something has been damaged beyond the hope of repair. Something is so damaged that nothing can be done. It means shattered, even crippled or maimed.

Brokenness is paradoxical because there are actually two types of responses or reactions to brokenness depending upon our perceptions. Either we choose to see our reality as God sees us and respond as a voluntary, broken Christian that uses brokenness to mature; or we choose to see our reality from a worldly, carnal perception and react as an involuntary, unbroken Christian that resists brokenness and remains immature. The two types of attitudes of brokenness depends on the level of intimacy and quality of our relationship with God, ourselves then others. Our perceptions, our beliefs and our behaviors must be in alignment with God's reality.

Involuntary brokenness is emotion reactionary living which resists the promptings and nudges of God for self-examination and blames everyone else or is harshly self-condemning. If a Christian gets stuck in the process and reacts with an involuntary posture their perception will cause them to be bitter, cynical, sarcastic, judgmental, filled with anger, a murmurer and complainer, a gossiper, critical, a backbiter and lead to an infectious wounded spirit.

My wounds were the sounds of involuntary brokenness: "Woe is me, I don't measure up. "I'll never amount to anything." "Nobody loves me, not even God." "Nobody will ever hurt me again." "If it wasn't for you, I would be..." "I can't stand her she makes me sick." "I'm tired of being overlooked, ignored and rejected." "What's the use, I'm tired." "I'm entitled to." "Why did they have to die?" "Life's not fair." I lived in the victim mentality but answered God's call to live in a new dimension to live beyond the average perception.

Voluntary brokenness is the spiritual response that is perceived as the process of building Christian character by reducing or breaking one to a humble, submissive state. This process is welcomed to examine, then penetrate, shatter and breakthrough the hardened perceptions and the belief system of the mind; to heal the damaged emotions; and gently nudges the indecisive will to make righteous choices and decisions.

Brokenness is recognized as God's requirement for human usefulness. Brokenness is also perceived as God's vehicles of transportation that drives us to our destiny. The desired outcomes are obedience, a better, trusting and loving attitude. The broken soul will undergo this process yielded and humbled and will continue to thrive and overcome despite everything they've gone through.

The sounds of voluntary brokenness are:" I don't like the pain, but I will praise God all the way through to receive the power." "I know that this is for my good, to prove and humble me." "I know that there is a lesson in this for me and principles that I need to apply." "I know that God loves me and He's helping me grow in grace right now." "Father, forgive them because forgiveness is the final form of love." "This is working together for my good, even though it doesn't feel good." "I'll be able to help others because there is purpose in this pain." "This is motivating me to hurry up and end one season of my life and begin a new season of development." "I'm going to make my pain pay me."

Brokenness is a matter of perception, choice and behavior:

1. Whether you see your new life in Christ through His love eyes through faith and choose to walk/behave according to the law of life in Christ Jesus
2. Whether you see your life through your past hurts and revert back to your old behavior before salvation and live a life as a faithless, mediocre Christian without purpose and passion and choose the law of sin and death. You always have choices.

You make the choice God makes the change.

Ecclesiastes 3 discusses times and seasons of life. Today, we live in a world that has just been shocked, ravished and devastated by a pandemic and God takes this brokenness and issues a call to hope. The hope is that God could restore that which is shattered. The hope is that God could do the impossible. We are surrounded by the reality of pain and problems and primarily experienced are three types of brokenness: 1) Physical Brokenness - injuries, illness, deaths, 2) Emotional Brokenness - hurts, griefs and sorrows that run deep, 3) Spiritual Brokenness - our sins or the sins of others such as racism, crimes, or abuse which leaves us broken. Which type of brokenness have you experienced the most?

I thought that I was completely whole after I published, Broken To Be Made Whole, over twenty-eight years ago; but, I took an X-ray and it revealed that I was only healed in some areas, still broken in other areas, and experienced depression, anxiety, questions, confusion, doubts and fears. Wondering how could this happen to me? I'm a Christian, a minister, a counselor and God used me to help others. I discovered the people that need to heal the most, believe that they are perfectly whole, as I did because we lack true humility. God removes the impurities from brokenness in our lives in layers, layer upon layer. According to Terry Wardle there are four layers that God heals one layer at a time. The deepest layer is the pain layer, then the protection layer, the provision layer and the punishment layer. Dr. Kevin K. Daniels revealed that there are three levels of trauma, acute trauma, chronic trauma and complex trauma. Just know there's always more, but God is faithful and knows what time and what season to, break and to make. Just don't ignore Him when He's tugging at your heart to convict you, not condemn you, or chasten you and not punish you.

Childhood toxic fear, anxiety and stress is real and is often the results of generational iniquities and sins of our fore father's which causes brokenness as an adult. Sfg. Bishop C. Shawn Tyson preached, "Fear, Stress and Anxiety are the Unholy Trinity. Many believers that deal with fear, stress and anxiety are unwilling to talk about it. Why, because we are spirit-filled believers filled with the Holy Ghost, and we are ashamed to admit we have fearful moments. Because we are more concerned about our image, we will suppress stress, mask anxiety and quote a scripture on fear trying to keep ourselves together and wonder why we aren't delivered. It's the environment of deceit which then gives the enemy the energy and unlawful entrance to wreak havoc in our lives for 10, 20, and 40, years while we are still sincerely quoting the scriptures and praying.

He continues in Psalms 66:18, "If, I regard iniquity in my heart the Lord will not hear me." If, I hold onto a worry, fear and deep pain and try to tuck it away in my heart knowing it's unresolved, and attempt to proceed forward, it's a sin. We ask, why won't God answer our prayers? Because effective prayer is not right words, but it's the right heart, spirit. If we desire for God to heal us holistically, we must be transparent….. If we don't deal with the unholy trinity it becomes a stronghold. You must be authentic with God. Perfect love cast out fear….."

He stated, in another message, "Sometimes God will allow us to be hurt to put us in a position to help others when we get tired and weary of helping. We get trapped in the spirit of selfishness. But we are obligated to pull others out with the same help we received. The less we think about fulfilling our needs, and the more we think about others, the more God will increase our resources when we are balanced. The most essential component of greatness is humility."

We can return to helping others once we are released. Many times the energies we expend in our performance behaviors can lead to the "chronic fatigue syndrome." It takes quiet, intentional, focused committed time, humility, surrender and sheer honesty to identify where you really are and where you need to go. Job 33:14 states, "For God speaketh once, yea, twice, yet man perceiveth it not. Listen to God.

I can still hear the voice of the late, Evangelist Mildred Boyd, saying, "You are blessed because you admit that you battle with fear, stress and anxiety. Saints can be some of the biggest liars, if they won't admit their battles with their inner struggles and cover them up with their gifts, talents, titles and anointing's."

This was relevant for me because decades later God requested that I'd share with a group of women at Metro Assemblies Women's Retreat, who purchased several copies of my book, Yes Lord, regarding yielding to the Lord.

God said, "Stop Living a Lie". It took years for me to understand that I was not truly the nice, little, peacemaker that I thought I was, but can be a passive, fearful peace-faker at times. Others, who people respected for their aggressive nature and perceived as strong, were really angry, peace-takers. I was trying to project an image that I was more spiritual than I actually was because I was trying to please people. God was teaching me to become an authentic peacemaker.

How do we know when we are broken? How do we know when we're whole? Bishop N.L. Wagner stated," Some of us have broken things in our lives and don't know it's broken. If a person is negative about someone they will be negative about you. They need to get an X-ray and get in spiritual alignment. They must consciously move from stress to rest. God can take what sin has marred and do something about it." God would continue to beckon me to Him in Isaiah 30:15, "In returning and rest shall ye be saved; in quietness and in confidence shall be your strength; and ye would not." During the Covid19 coronavirus pandemic in 2020, we were summons to self-examination, x-rays and away from stress to rest. God spared our lives.

Many of us sincerely love God and are good Christians, saints and believers, but the shift today and clarion call from God is for all of His children that He created in His image and likeness before the foundation of the world, to come higher into a new dimension in love, come forth and come alive. God wants godly, mature sons and daughters who are revived from their lukewarm state and busyness, driven by doing good works, to just stop and be present in Him. It's a call to return to your first love in Him.

Once, a Bishop of our organization and a well-known evangelist stated, while buying one of my revised versions of Broken to Be Made Whole, said that he was supporting me, but he didn't read, nor need books like this. He continued and stated because he was a Bishop that He only read deep books. He would donate it to someone who needs this information.

God quickly revealed to me, "How saddened I am with my people who don't recognize that some of them are broken cisterns filled with holes. Some of my people have bleeding, heartbreaking, unconscious childhood protective patterns which are spiritual blockages and ungodly motivations that are still hidden in their hearts. Yes, they are saved, yes I use them, but they are still unaware of these hidden patterns and all of their ministries, titles, accomplishments, status, wealth, humanitarian deeds, power, popularity and any other worldly attempts to heal will be temporary band aids. There will always be a need to examine themselves daily, then repent. I'm standing here in you and they are passing me by. I am offering him a chance to heal from the spirit of pride and he would not heed."

Pastor Tyson taught Five Emotional Lessons Learned From Elijah, the Prophet:

1. Spiritual brilliance does not automatically equate to emotional balance.
2. Our relationship with God is not designed to take the place of our relationships with our family and our friends.
3. Being a great Pastor, Prophet or Priest will not in and of itself make you a complete or emotionally balanced person.
4. Doing right by God will not stop people from doing wrong by you.
5. We must always balance our feelings with our faith, faith is not balanced by our emotions.

Think back to the time when we first became a Christian, a believer, a saint, then perhaps promoted as a Christian leader. We were promoted because of the intimate relationship we developed with God and manifested the fruit of the spirit of God. We were loving, kind, peaceful, hopeful and whole in our hearts, secure in the love for our Lord, God and Savior, Jesus Christ. Our initial motivations in service were pure and we loved everybody. God's love was our motivation and our intentions were undefiled, sincere and pure. We were idealist and zealous with high hopes, with dreams and visions regarding our newfound love, Jesus. We had a hunger and thirst after righteousness and a sincere desire to be filled with righteousness.

When we were witnessed to, we were told once we were reconciled back to God, we'd never have any more problems. The truth is, once we're saved we no longer serve Satan, and he launches spiritual attacks in our minds to attempt to discredit God and weaken our faith. When we encountered unexpected wounds, brokenness, unexpected losses, setbacks, train wrecks, obstacles, hurdles, betrayals and pain, we experienced a crisis of our faith and were distracted. Some began to increase our works and busyness to attempt to be holier and earn God's favor, but it's a heart issue. Has your heart been broken to the things of God?

Christians do experience dilemmas, battling with self-righteousness and hidden sins of the heart within. Physical or emotional struggles are always going to shake us. God is constant and unchanging. He is the anchor we grasp by faith when everything threatens to overwhelm us. In Romans 7, Paul was greatly used by God because he admitted he still needed to be ministered to in his broken places, as he ministered to others.

Dr. Shawn Carr so eloquently ministered a message recently regarding King David's brokenness. King David was a man after God's own heart because he repented when God showed him his heart and prayed for a clean heart. King David's generational iniquities was filled with sexual sins that affected him and his family for five and six generations. However, King David had the answer. He wrote, in Psalms 51:5-6, "Behold, I was shapen in iniquity; and in sin did my mother conceive me -thou desirest truth in the inward parts." Now King David prays as he continues his communion with the Lord in Psalms 51:10 and prays, "Create in me a clean heart and renew a right sprit within me." David identifies the greatest cause of our struggles, the enemy within ourselves. He didn't blame God, nor others or circumstances or ignore God's promptings because he was the King. He never used excuses, but acknowledged that every last one of us was born in sin and must be willing to come clean. The key, the answer, to the question, has your heart been broken to the things of God? Is it a clean heart?

The only way to possess a clean heart is found in Psalms 51:17, The sacrifices of God are a broken and contrite spirit. So having a contrite heart means "to be broken, crushed" and having a heart that recognizes our sinfulness, pride, arrogance, self-hatred and brokenness. It also means being humble and teachable. It means hitting bottom and realizing that only God and following His way can turn things around for us. Being crushed, bruised and broken is a prerequisite for being restored, healed, forgiven and transformed. If we approach Him contritely, He can create in us pure, sound, loving, peaceful hearts that will rejoice forevermore.

It is imperative to discern that these experiences were part of the process where God uses pain and brokenness to tear down our false belief systems (lies), break up our fallow ground, character defects, destroy our childhood protective patterns, and unhealthy relationship attachment patterns. He then builds up our character by renewing our mind, healing our damaged emotions, identifying and releasing damaging spiritual roots, and conform us to the image of Christ with His Truth. However, during a process of time, without moving from faith to faith, strength to strength, glory to glory and maintaining great meekness and humility; we slowly experienced an unconscious shift from God-centered living back to self-centered living, trying to protect ourselves from our hurts through busyness.

While working and serving the Lord, the little foxes of our soul that has been subjected to all sorts of unconscious, negative self-inflicted wounds or other inflicted wounds, and stress must be identified, broken and destroyed. We may slowly drift back to how the world defines us as successful and lose our identity in God. Our own unconscious proclivities that create an environment can adversely impact us and that's when God proceeds to break us to make us. Other times we are masking our emotions because of our traditions and beliefs that don't allow any weaknesses and show of emotions, especially in leadership.

Psalms 147:2-3, "The Lord doth build up Jerusalem: He gathereth together the outcasts of Israel. He healeth the broken in heart, and bindeth up their wounds." Brokenness is a paradox and perhaps one of the most misunderstood principles. Brokenness is part of the human condition. We are surrounded by the reality of pain and problems and because we are now spiritual beings still living in a fleshly body, it can become challenging until we overcome the worldly perception of brokenness and perceive God's Reality.

I believe that most Christians don't want to or refuse to perceive themselves as broken people, but none of us avoid a broken heart. Nevertheless, guarded hearts even get broken. Broken hearts are part of life in the fallen, broken world.

The best intentioned mothers, like mine and others, tried to mend our hearts when we were young, buy treats or take special trips to the store or to the movies. With good intentions and deep desires, they try to fix their child's broken heart. The pain can lessen or be momentarily forgotten with the physical distractions, but the brokenness remains. Adults use the same diversions to numb the pain of their broken hearts: food, alcohol, drugs, sex, shopping, pornography, social media, etc. Again the surface pain can be forgotten temporarily, but the deeper brokenness remains. We all have hurts. We don't let go of the wounds very easy because the wounds are very deep, but faith and obedience through a process of time, will unlayer the hidden man of the heart and eventually catapult us into the spiritual realm above the pain. God heals those who are afflicted with griefs and troubles.

How do we get over the pain? How does God heal our broken hearts? How does God fix our wounded spirits? How do we receive clean hearts? How can we testify that we are broken, but for the last time?

Here, in the text, Psalms 147:3, imagine this, picture this. Jesus is the Great Physician and Christians (Israelites) are the patients in the spiritual hospital, the true church of the living God. These patients who are being rolled in the hospital on gurneys have two conditions, brokenness of heart and wounded spirits. These two conditions seem synonymous because both terms indicate distress, and in some interpretations of this text, they are perceived as one condition. I would like to note it is possible that there are some differences. Whether they are one in the same condition or different the symptomatic conditions must be X-rayed and acknowledged before they can be resolved. The broken heart can be healed and the wounded spirit needs the divine grace and mercy that only God can touch. Let's take an honest look at the voluntary broken in heart like King David:

1. Acknowledgment of wrong. A person with a broken spirit does not make excuses or blame others. He takes full responsibility for his wrongdoing or healing from the wrongdoing of others.
2. Contrition. A broken spirit produces genuine sorrow.
3. Humility. Self-will has been shattered, there is no attempt to lift oneself up.
4. Seeking after God. The person with a broken spirit has faced his own poverty and sin. He has no righteousness of his own to promote, but rather, he seeks to know God.
5. Teach ability. He is done with his own answers to life and is ready to turn to the Lord for help. He does not want his problem explained or justified, but simply wants help to change.
6. Godly Unworthiness. This person who is broken in spirit does not demand, he asks. His focus is not on getting all that he

> deserves, but he is grateful instead of complaining. He has tasted mercy and is done with demanding rights.

A broken spirit makes a person a joy to be around. He has a tenderness in manner, a gratitude for what others do, a humility about himself, and a gentleness in relating to others who have faults. God is nigh to the broken and God heals the broken in heart.

Brokenness of heart presupposes that our hearts were whole at one time i.e. Adam and Eve, before the fall of man, and sin. When we were born again we have whole hearts towards God because our sins are washed away and we are reconciled back to God in peace. But sins and fiery darts that attacked, broke and pierced our hearts must be plucked out of the heart. So the Master Physician begins the spiritual surgical procedures on their hearts.

There are many baby boomers today who have been sexually violated by trusted high profile individuals in every aspect and walk of life, the church, entertainment, media, sports, politics etc. who are now seeking healing and establishing movements based upon their experiences of misuse and abuse. I want to take this opportunity to invite you to Jesus in the fullness of the Godhead. He has something more for you. Let Him heal you, too!

Christians (Israel's) broken hearts were inflicted by their evil environment. Of course, Israel wept bitter tears because of the sorrow, shame, and anguish they felt as they reflected on their past lives and rebellion against a righteous God. But, God promised that "He heals the broken in heart and binds up their wounds."

The condition to the promise is that we must admit that we are broken, bring all of the pieces to Him and depend on Him to heal us. Addictions are indicators that we are attempting to heal ourselves.

Heal, In Hebrew, "Raphe", means to heal, to sew together, or mend.

Heart, defined in Hebrew is "lev or levav" refers to more than our emotions, but our thoughts and spiritual life. The heart was viewed as the center of everything for a person. The heart was the source of the will, the conscience and determination. The heart was the place of strength and the place of courage within a person's life. The heart is the seat of our emotions, our spiritual character. The physical heart is an organ positioned to protect the body and give life by pumping blood, likewise, the spiritual heart must be guarded for our spiritual health and wellness.

The broken heart means to have the core of one's being crushed. The implications of being brokenhearted is extreme. Brokenhearted means to have everything that makes a person who they are, ripped from them. Brokenhearted means to have courage and strength torn from a life in a violent manner.

Bind defined in Hebrew, "chabash" means to bind, bind on or bind up, wrap around tightly as wrapping a bandage around a wound.

Wounds defined in Hebrew, "makkah or makkeh" means a blow, word or slaughter. In Hebrew, the understanding of wounds is much broader than we think. Being wounded meant to experience injury of any kind or to experience any kind of pain. A breach of the skin and flesh. Being wounded is to be filled with sorrow, to be hurt or to experience trouble. A wound is to hurt by violence.

We all have hidden wounds. Isaiah 1:5-6, "....the whole head is sick, and the heart faint. From the sole of the foot even unto the head there is no soundness in it; but wounds, bruises, and putrefying sores; they have not been closed, neither bound up, neither mollified with ointment."

Wounds are often troubles and memories of the conscience.

A wounded spirit in Proverbs 17:22 a broken spirit drieth the bones, and in Proverbs 18:14, the spirit of a man will sustain his infirmity; but a wounded spirit who can bear it. It refers to a crushed spirit. A wounded spirit is one that is hurting, but one in which the hurt has festered into an unbearable attitude and negative responses.

A person with a wounded spirit, involuntary brokenness lives in inner misery that focuses regularly on his injuries and results in the following:

1. A negative mind-set. The person with the negative mindset is preoccupied with past injuries. He views incidents in the worst light. He sees the bad and ignores the good. His mind is filled with woes, suspicion and assumption of evil.
2. Victim reasoning. With a wounded spirit, a person views himself as a sufferer. He can turn even kind actions of others into additional grievances, into added pain in his life.
3. Blame tactics. A person with a wounded spirit holds other people responsible for the misery in their life.
4. Grievance mannerisms. Out of a wounded spirit come sighs, groans, and exclamations that draw attention to their hurt. Acting out the symptoms of their pain.

Proverbs asks, A wounded spirit who can bear? Out of the wounds oozes the stench of self-pity, bitterness, and accusations. It is difficult to live with anyone who has a wounded spirit. God identifies the spiritual roots behind brokenness and mental illness. God uproots the lies of self-accusation, self-introspection, and self-centeredness, shame, guilt and self-pity and stops you from reliving your past by bringing it into the present. He replenishes the serotonin that is depleted in patients who do not feel loved and accepted. He resets the chemical and hormonal imbalance by healing the hypothalamus and other parts of the limbic system that are affected that are responsible for regulating mood, thinking, sleep, appetite and behavior that was manipulate by the enemy through our thoughts.

God heals or sews together the broken, shattered, fragmented, and violently torn, damaged heart, the essence of our identity our courage and strength; and binds up, tightly wraps a bandage around the wounds, breached and broken flesh, injury and hurt that is filled with sorrow. He heals the core of who we are by reminding us that we are accepted in the beloved. We are the apple of His eye. We are somebody because we are God's body.

God wraps us up in His love. He tightly covers the open flesh or bleeding hearts that have taken out the rejection as we choose to replace it with acceptance; He uproots the anger and bitterness and helps us to choose forgiveness. He eradicates the worry, fear and anxiety and strengthens us to choose to walk in the peace of God that passes all understanding. He takes the abuse and misuse and turns it into a useful testimony for His Glory. He takes out the labels, nicknames, name calling and curses that demeaned our very existence and piles up love and endearing words to erase any negativity and replaces it with an identity in Him. He cleanses the infection from the oozing puss that has made us septic and almost near death with mega doses of love. He wraps us up in His affection, affirmation, appreciation, comfort, encouragement respect and support as we are snuggled in His bosom.

Personally, I was confronted with several truths at once that stirred up hidden emotions that needed to come to the surface. It was necessary for these fears and anxieties to surface because I had become so toxic from past hurts, that I had infections, inflammations and poisons backing up in my body. In God's infinite wisdom and timing, I took my X-ray at Meier Christian Counseling Clinic when I was diagnosed with a thyroid disease, anxiety, depression, bi-polar II, panic disorder, Add/Adhd, and the list goes on. I was immediately admitted to the outpatient clinic and Luther and I resided in the clinic hotel in Battle Creek, Michigan for four weeks. I was "burnt out" physically, emotionally, mentally and spiritually. I experienced intensive training and therapy and began learning how damaged emotions turn into disease.

What you feel emotionally becomes how you feel physically. The body can't differentiate between stress that physical factors cause and stress that emotional factors cause. Stress is stress. Stress is the body and mind's response to any pressure that disrupts their normal balance. It occurs when our perceptions of events don't meet our expectations and we don't manage our reaction to the disappointment. Stress unmanaged expresses itself as tension, frustration, strain, resistance and throws off our physiological and psychological equilibrium. The body releases chemicals that occur at the cellular level and effect the organs. God revealed that busyness exposed me to experiencing an addiction to the elevated levels of adrenaline and cortisol.

The continued cycle of adrenaline/cortisol and fatigue cycle without the rest was tearing my body and every system in my body down. Elevated levels of adrenaline over time can also cause blood to clot faster, the thyroid to become overstimulated, the body to produce more cholesterol, impair immune function, impair memory, reduce glucose, increase fat accumulation, reduce muscle mass and eventually become deadly, if left unmanaged. Those who are addicted to the stress hormones are often very successful in their careers because they are always pushing themselves to achieve new goals that will give them a temporary emotional high.

Adrenaline, the feel-good hormone, from stress, eventually becomes addictive. I was no different than a person who came off drugs or alcohol. I had severe withdrawal symptoms, BUT GOD promised, "He heals the broken in heart and binds up their wounds." To heal the heart I learned King David's another secret to a clean heart is found in Psalms 42:5, "Why is thy soul cast down, why is my soul disquieted within me? Hope in God, for I shall yet praise Him for the help of His countenance. "Self-Talk" is a tremendous tool for healing your soul:

1. Admit to yourself what you are feeling
2. Make the verbal choice to hope in God
3. Acknowledge God is near, nigh to the broken in heart. It is important during times of stress to turn from yourself to God, admit your feelings, cast your concerns on Him, and voice your decision to trust Him. When healing your heart you need quiet, effective communication to receive the internal nudge or sense of warning.

The intense and comprehensive teachings on "Life Skills such as Anger Management, Assertiveness, Boundaries, Beliefs, Codependency, Feelings, Forgiveness, Identity in Christ and Stress Management greatly improved my quality of life.

There were wounded pastors, pastors wives, school teachers and persons struggling with co- dependencies in the church. I was touched by the transparency and compassion of our Christian therapists and desired to follow their example of administering grace then truth. I believe many "church hurts" occurred because there needs to be a balance of compassion and truth. They opened our eyes to the truth that we weren't free from all of the iniquity and sin in our lives. We still had so much stuff buried deep within us that we believed we could overcome in spite of it. But they taught us that we were overcomers when we dealt with it. Our church leaders can administer doses of truth, the scriptures, only after they have taken the time to be compassionate by listening with a spiritual ear.

Denial of emotional needs is the most common problem hindering a person from healing and being made whole. Denying your needs will lead to: pride, self-reliance, self-sufficiency, a stony heart, becoming shut-off, needy, looking for love in the wrong places, emptiness and loneliness.

We identified our unmet childhood needs; the lies we believed when they weren't met; the lies we built into our thinking patterns; suppressed and regressed emotions; inappropriate behaviors and applied truth as we renounced the lies. The biggest lie we had in common was believing that because people rejected us we were inadequate, unworthy and unloved. We replaced it with the truth of the matter.

Acceptance means we are no longer forsaken or rejected; we no longer believe lies and know that we are accepted in Him. We learned many churches are codependent and either their members leave or they force their pastor and his/her family to leave wounded because they failed to teach boundaries. The experience at the Meier's Clinic was just the beginning of a long process of unlayering 50 plus years of brokenness, but I was used to restore a backslidden school teacher and renew hope in several clients. God was assigning me to clinical work without a clinical degree.

Ten years later I was admitted to the Chronic Pain Clinic at the Cleveland Clinic after suffering with fibromyalgia for years. Once again I was taught the roots of certain mind-body-spirit diseases. Fibromyalgia is rooted in suppressed anger and after four weeks of releasing suppressed and repressed feelings, I was discharged and never had fibromyalgia again. I wasn't given any medication to treat it except Cymbalta for a few days which I discontinued. It was the consistent release from suppressed and repressed feelings from my heart for years and replacing them with the truth.

During this time we developed a friendship with a couple from Columbus and I was able to lead my friend Melody's husband, Mark, to the Lord. He was baptized in Jesus Name and filled with the Holy Ghost on April 17, 2016 at Messias Temple Church. He had severe chronic pains and was delivered in November 2020 at a revival in their church. Each clinic stay was intentional and on purpose because lives were changed, souls were saved and God received the glory from my story. I was no longer ashamed of the gospel of Jesus Christ in the mental health facilities. I was called to "heal the broken hearted."

During this time I prayed for a healing in my brain and memory, and asked God to help me continue to be broken, but for the last time. He helped me face my past in the light of His love, for the last time, as He takes the pain out of the memory. We resolve to make the choice to change and God makes the change. He took the pain out of the memory, helped me to face it for the last time, and give me a miracle in my memory. The memory will retain the experience either consciously but more than often unconsciously, but I knew that I was healed when I still remember past traumas without the pain in the memory.

The seventh step is to request a miracle in our memory because the spirit makes intercession (goes underground) for our infirmities (personality quirks). We make the choice to change and God makes the change. The healing of the memory restores God's image, removes the power of those who hurt us and, in turn, gives us freedom from bondage to our past says Derek Overly, author of Issues of the Soul.

1. The mind is healed by thinking right thoughts,
2. The emotions are healed by dealing with the past.
3. The will is healed by making right choices. Those choices have got to be God's choice. His will must become our will.
4. Then we will see a total healing of the spirit, soul, and body. The victory is won or lost by the mind."

Resolve brings you to heart issues. When I settle in my heart the ways of God, then I'm no longer moved by my emotions. Other people are no longer my source of approval and acceptance and I no longer listen to lies. "Life is a gift, but, living requires life skills, an art form." N.L.W. We don't live life by our emotions. It has nothing to do with our feelings, but we live by obedience to the truth and dispel lies. The battle is with principalities, powers, spiritual wickedness in high places, and thoughts that didn't come from God. We are led by the spirit, not our emotions. My wounds were finally opened and the bacteria was released from my body. Eventually, everything which is hidden will come into the light. My thoughts were no longer interfering with my spiritual desires and health, but were being exposed layer by layer.

We must be able to recognize the childhood protective patterns and give them to God and ask Him to re-parent any area of parental negligence or ignorance. He removes the negative, destructive labels, words, and acts of bullying and rocks you in His lap and changes your perception of a cold, distant, absent father, until you lay your head on His chest and cry Abba, Father, Daddy, Daddy. He is the multi-breasted one who gently pours, nourishing unconditional love down our throats and allows it to soothe us inside. We are responsible to swallow and digest His healing balm to heal us. He prescribes mega doses of gospel pills to be taken at least three times daily. What is your prescription?

We are responsible to allow the stitches to hold the wounds together by not ripping them apart in times of stress or fits of anger. Leave the bandages on that He wraps around our wounds to heal until He instructs us to remove them. We can't see the stitches, but our faith must believe that He is at work on the inside of our bodies. He is working from the inside and teaching us to live from the inside out by removing the opinions of others that were lodged on the inside and have no use in our memories. He is at work sewing us back together again stitch by stitch, without the negative input, so over time we will receive our complete healing.

Jesus, the visible manifestation of the invisible God, robed in the flesh and walked the earth as a human example to show us how to live a holy life. He was rejected. He was wounded, bruised, beaten and scourged for our sins as well as an example of suffering and brokenness, for the salvation of the masses. He endured a crown of thorns which was thrust into his head; huge spikes were driven through his hands and feet; He endured severe beatings and had thirty-nine stripes on His back, and felt the sharp pierce of a sword jabbed through His side, which shed the water and the blood for the cleansing of our sins. He could identify with our wounds. He knows what it feels like to be betrayed, forsaken by those closest to you, and left alone.

The Lord God is a Master Physician, a healer, who is the only one who can restore the broken. Remember that Jesus is right there to bring us through it. He's there to give us hope and increase our faith. Even in our state of brokenness, He's still doing a good work in us. Though it doesn't look or feel so good in the beginning of our crisis, the end is going to be so much better. When you are broken, it's time to draw nearer to God to seek Him for direction, clarity, help and strength. Please identify the areas where you're no longer broken in because God has completely healed you.

I'm no longer taking twenty-two medications daily. I am still medicated for high blood pressure and occasionally medication for constipation. No longer afflicted with fibromyalgia, acid reflux, pre-diabetes, neuropathy, bi-polar, depression, unworthiness, inadequacies, feeling unloved nor inferior. There are areas that I'm yet believing God for, But God is faithful.

Can't you hear the chains falling? The breakthroughs changed the sounds and words to "I am enough in God." "God is Love." "Life isn't fair, But God is a righteous judge." "It's not my sister or brother, but the spirit and principality that I'm standing against, but I am standing." "I forgive them because they don't even know what they are doing." "I'm not ignored, hidden or invisible, but a secret weapon hidden." "I'm not tired, The Lord has strengthened me." "A quitter never wins and a winner never quits." "The only excuse to quit is death." "My season has changed and I'm making the adjustment by reinventing myself." "Loved ones will leave us and we honor them by living in our purpose."

I never knew that I was wounded and under the bondage of a principality called "an unloving spirit" until it was revealed at an, Be In Health, Overcomers Conference recently. My mind was renewed as I was able to discern, understand, gain knowledge, and wisdom regarding the hidden spirit that I allowed to rule my entire life. I shifted from a lifetime of bondage into His good pleasure. Immediately, I knew that I was loved, and able to choose good from evil and walked in the spirit of peace. I was able to completely heal from multiple losses of close friends through deaths and life's circumstances.

As the good physician, He has deep sympathy for everyone who has lost loved ones and grieving. Those of us in mourning receive special attention and extra doses of His goodness and His Love. St. Matthew states, "Blessed are they that mourn for they shall be comforted." Mourning is the outward expression of that loss. It is a process that helps the bereaved make sense of the end of a loved one's life and gives structure to what can feel like a very confusing time. Time helps heal all wounds, but God heals all wounds, if we let Him.

He continues to reassure us in Hebrews 13:5....for he hath said, I will never leave thee, nor forsake thee. God's promises are always before us and never behind us enabling us to move in our expectation. Mourning becomes therapeutic when we can face reality, accept our loss, and readjust to living without our loved ones. Our tears become liquid prayers that he bottles up and pours out into joy.

During my grief, when Sherlyn was murdered over nineteen years ago, self-pity over took me and invaded my mind initially. An emotional wound coupled with the underlying spirit of self-pity rushed in, invaded my mind and it became unsound. One Sunday night during our ministers meeting, called Shepherd's Hour, Bishop Wagner said, "Cheryl tell the ministers about your friend that was murdered.

I shared with them that Sherlyn and I were friends for over thirty-five years when we met at Mumford High School as juniors. When we graduated she attended Central Michigan University and I attended Eastern Michigan. She was transferring to Eastern the year I flunked out, and she remained at Central. I asked her if she was interested in joining the Detroit Police Department with me. We both passed our physicals, but she passed the written test that I failed. She remained on the force for twenty-five years then retired, and I surrendered my life to Jesus and was born again. Even though there were times I felt like I failed in my worldly goals, I continued to witness to my friend for over twenty years. She was baptized at Straight gate Apostolic Church in

Detroit, Michigan while providing security for the pastor, Bishop Andrew Merritt and filled with the Holy Ghost. She'd just accepted her call to prison ministry and loved it. She called me a few weeks before Valentine's Day 2001 thanked me for being an example, for writing anointed, powerful books and leading her to the Lord. She was truly born again.

One week later when I received the call from my mother that Sherlyn was dead, I screamed so loudly that my entire apartment complex could hear me. She had been retired for two years and never harmed on her job, but was murdered as a patron in a Dry Cleaners during a robbery. To date they have never arrested her murderer. It's a Cold Case.

After I shared the story, Bishop said, "And you've never been the same since. I was never the same." The grief opened the door for the unlawful entrance to ungodly spirits to wreak havoc in my life no matter how hard I tried to regain my spiritual walk with God. I healed when God reminded me He saved her soul and He used my testimony and life as a witness to her. He also reminded me of The Nothing Book that she seeded into my life that turned into Broken To Be Made Whole and multiplied into numerous books, pamphlets and workbooks that will always soothe and comfort my heart and others.

Years later, when my father, my pastor, my friends Bernie, Vivian and Betty died so closely after Kathy, and other family members, friends and saints too numerous to list because of the pandemic, there was a difference. This time I was grieving, but free from the spirit of self-pity and I healed much quicker. It is possible to grieve for a loss and still keep yourself from losing the perspective and appreciation for the good things that remain in your life. Self-pity was another spirit that had to be broken and the yoke destroyed. I participated with God and started choking out this principality of an unloving spirit with the Word of God.

Colossians 1:12-13 states, "Giving thanks unto the Father, which hath made us meet to be partakers of the inheritance of the saints in light: Who hath delivered us from the power of darkness, and hath translated us into the kingdom of His dear Son."

Our expectation of healing must be greater than our pain and devastation. When the door has been closed in one area of our lives, God has opened another door for a new beginning in other areas of our lives as He exposes Light. It's easier said than done and we must engage in spiritual warfare to overcome these ungodly spirits.

When our spirit was broken with grief, Satan tries to get a foothold to come in like a thief and attempts to steal our worth and identity, kill our faith and joy in who we are, destroy our dreams and the life that we had hoped for, and to have us emotionally beaten down to the point where we go from being who we were to someone who had lost all hopes. No matter what broken state we are in, we are never beyond God's reach. We are never so far gone that God can't make us effective for His purposes. I had to give Him every broken piece of my heart and watch the Great Physician masterfully perform surgery on me. That was Light. There is a Morning after Our Mourning, a poem I wrote that is in my book, Broken, But Look at Me Now, that was inspired by my grieving process.. Since Covid19 we've experienced multiple losses of friends and were unable to attend their funerals which was very painful, But God granted closure.

Few people will associate with those who experience chronic long term pain and mental illnesses, but God abides, hangs out with us, stays with us and actually chooses our company. God hangs out and hovers over the bi-poplars. He has help for us whether we are living in our manic episode of great elation or the alternate episode at the other end of the pole of sadness. While living in the extreme high or mania one day with great courage, confident, and displaying risk-taking behaviors that provides unlimited energy and sleepless nights for days; or the depressive episodes that lands you in a deep, dark hole for days, in the bed, under the covers in a spiraling, dismal hole with no daylight in sight. He is there and provides a safe place of peace to prevent the disorder from manifesting again.

When a person does feel safe, loved or accepted, their body responds by reducing the excessive amount of serotonin which caused the additional chemical imbalances. The neurotransmitter imbalances will return to normal and you will no longer have bipolar disorder because the foundation of an unloving spirit, the feeling of not being accepted, and of being driven to find something to take the place of that lack of acceptance is gone. The mania is often a fixation on achievement, where people are driven in some uncontrollable way toward success.

God has a relationship with the sick, with the wretched and the wounded as He walks the halls of the hospital of the church. He's breaking those spiritual bondages and chains of our childhood protective patterns, and defense mechanisms. He will never leave us nor forsake us. He heals and comforts us. He specializes in handling and healing the broken hearts. He applies the ointment of grace and the soft bandages of love and binds up our bleeding hearts and wounds one stitch at a time. He is so longsuffering. He teaches us how to outlive our worldly, carnal experiences that were ingrained in our brains, how to reach up into the spiritual realm to defeat the opposing forces that kept us bound most of our lives' and be released into His Love.

He is the lover of our soul and woos us, kisses us and talks sweet words of love to us, conveying how He sees us through His love eyes. He sees us as altogether lovely, the apple of His eye, and precious in His sight. As the "apple of His eye" it means that the very focus of His attention is right on us and He's administering extreme care and protection because we are dearest to Him.

He provokes me to chase after Him even during weary times because He constantly reminds me that I am His beloved and He is the lover of my soul. He tends to the garden of my heart and picks out the weeds of abuse to preserve the beauty of my heart and the integrity and motivations of my heart.

He dismantles my excuses that I'm too sick. When people think that I am crazy, too fragile or too unassuming and laid back, or too hyper to be used, He offers relief, restoration and healing. But, we must show Him our brokenness and invite Him into the pain. God doesn't love like human beings. His love is unconditional, and He isn't afraid of my anxiety, bi-polar or brokenness. He doesn't make bi-polar jokes. He doesn't have unrealistic expectations of my abilities and performance during my episodes. He qualifies me and hides me in His strength.

He showed me that unresolved angry is a motivating force of anxiety. He broke the principality of the unloving spirit when He shed light on the scripture that I've read for years. Perfect love casts out fear meaning He'll send in an Intensive Care Team almost miraculously to administer mega doses of love until I learned how to love myself unconditionally. It's supernatural especially if your local hospital is low on their doses because they are battle fatigued. It's similar to the Red Cross sending donated blood. God has a trained staff of spiritual, sensitive mental health providers who have the spirit of God from a biblical perspective, who know how to treat others and bear our burdens. They are unselfish givers, not givers and takers. Spiritual people prioritize the needs of others and risk themselves for others. They demonstrate love and edify others.

Other assemblies within our community may have to lend a helping hand in extending grace if our warriors and soldiers are still wounded and in intensive care themselves. This perfect love of God engulfed me for at least three to five years in the most unlikely places and unique ways to heal my broken-heart. He will extend a clarion call to move people off of their jobs if need be for your sakes as He did for me. God showed me the responsible way to bind up my wounds was to stop and pray, wait on His Words of comfort and direction and resolve the issue in peace after the ungodly spiritual roots were cast back to dry places.

I would conclude this lesson from the text, with a supporting scripture in Isaiah 61:1, "The Spirit of the Lord God is upon me; because the Lord hath anointed me to preach good tidings unto the meek; He hath sent me to bind up the brokenhearted, to proclaim liberty to the captives, and the opening of the prison to them that are bound."

The church is the information highway standing between Heaven and Hell. The church has the authority and responsibility to fulfill the mission that Isaiah prophesied by revelation of the mazes, phases and crisis of their brothers and sisters.

He has issued a clarion call for ministers who can lead Christians by the Old Testament law to "break up their fallow ground and by the New Testament gospel "to rend their hearts."

The body, the soul (mind, emotions and will) and spirit are linked together. Begin to unravel the maze. How we feel emotionally can determine how we feel physically and live spiritually. Regardless of what we experience as believing Christian saints, we have been given dominion over the earth and we have authority and dominion in our prayers. Abiding in heavenly realms we speak to spirits and the spirt inside of us maketh intercession for our infirmities and others.

Infirmity here is not referring to our physical illnesses or diseases. Its reference is made regarding our personality quirks or those of others. The spirit must go underground and break up the fallow or hardened ground of our hearts and release the hidden root cause of the stronghold that keeps the Christian captured.

When you're, Broken to Be Made Whole, you must acknowledge that you are broken and identify the areas. After you identify your breaking points, defined as the moment of the greatest pain, stress, strain or crisis, at which something or someone breaks old outdated patterns, and lies are exposed. Embrace your breakthrough.

Breakthroughs defined are instances of achieving success and victory by releasing the past. Renew your mind by embracing new patterns, the truth of God's Word, to renew developmental patterns for change occur.

The beauty of brokenness is when God is stripping, breaking, cleansing, circumcising, sanctifying, shaping, molding, and transforming us to gain spiritual maturity. You will always feel like you're at a breaking point before you experience a breakthrough because you are forced to let go of old, comfortable, outdated attitudes, thoughts, habits and behaviors to receive new.

The only thing that mattered was living a life that celebrates the love God has given you and me. I was ready for my breakthrough to the new me.

CHAPTER 8
BREAKTHROUGH TO THE NEW YOU

I can still hear the words echoing in my spirit, "Brand New, brand new, brand new, God's going to make us brand new. I believe what the Bible says, God is going to make us brand new." These were prophetic words to an anointed song that Elder Darnell Thomas sang weekly, forty-five years ago, at Messias Temple during our praise services. I believe Darnell wrote that song and those words were divinely inspired by the scripture in II Cor. 5:17, "Therefore, if any man be in Christ, he is a new creature: old things are passed away; behold all things are become new."

Patty Scahill writes in her book, Mirror in the Word, "To be a new creature is to have the newness manifested in our spirit, speech, character, conduct, plans, purposes and desires. As we yield to Him, the remodeling of our "house" begins to take place." She makes reference to II Corinthians 3:18, But we all having an open face beholding as in a glass the glory of the Lord, are changed into the same image from glory to glory, even as, by the Spirit of the Lord. God made us as whole people, in His image (Genesis 1:27). That image includes physical, emotional, intellectual, social and relational dimensions.

In this season of Dimensional Exchange, A New Dimension in Love, God is blessing us where we were created to be in Him in the beginning. I can no longer live beneath my God-given privilege or inheritance. I refuse to be hidden in anxiety and depression. God created us as whole persons (spirit, soul and body) and we can no longer as spirit-filled believers ignore the soul and body. Ignoring any aspect of who we are as men and women made in God's image always results in destructive consequences in our ability to relate to God, with others, and with ourselves. God is issuing a clarion call to shift into a dimensional exchange, from our old perception into the perception and character of God. God has a plan for our lives, but He won't do it through the old you. He wants an update. He has a new role and a new assignment which requires replacing old broken language and sounds with speaking God's Words of life.

When I began to seek God for new thoughts and revelations for progressive movements in the area of Mental Health and the church, He instructed me to define the word new.

Webster defines the word new as knowledge that was not known before or recently discovered knowledge that produces a change. New is likened unto the renovation process of anything that needed to be repaired. New is also defined as something that was there all the time, but has been recently just discovered.

The Greek word for new is kainos, defined as meaning fresh. Its reference is in the sense of a fresh understanding that draws a contrast to the old. To be "Woke", as the young people say today.

Oh, now I understand! My purpose, my identity and my image is restored. I've always been complete and whole because I am created in His image and likeness. Wholeness has been inside of me, but I've just discovered what God revealed about me. My journey in brokenness has shifted me from living a defensive, emotional reactionary life of fighting rejection, depression, anxiety, bi-polar II, and other stress-related illnesses to unearth a new, fresh, loving perspective and perception regarding my experiences in life. I was gifted with ability to hear God's voice but I failed to give Him a proper response according to His Character of Love, Light and Spirit. God revealed that my new identity in Him, my new purpose and the new perception was there all the time, hidden in the beauty of brokenness. I learned that I will never develop without pain because pain is inevitable, but misery is optional. There is purpose in our pain.

My deliverance and development was not solely in the blessings, but in the brokenness which is the preparation for the dimensional exchange, deployment, promotion and elevation in love.

The contrast is, just because I had a broken heart, didn't mean that I was a broken person like I was in the eyes of the world. But, I was broken unto the things of God. He wept through me, touched the hearts of others through me and used me to minister HOPE to others. Just because I was diagnosed with multiple mental illnesses according to the Diagnostic Statistical Manual for Mental Health (DSM) and learned broken relationship patterns during childhood, didn't mean I was a bad, negative, worthless, unloving person. Neither was I crazy or a person with a bad mind. I just needed to learn how to celebrate the love that God gave me by using the experiences to grow and mature in God and help others more than ever today. What a difference a day makes.

I'm sure God used our church services, Bible classes, traditional methods of revivals, conferences, convocations, women's retreats, conventions, vacations and mental health clinics to deliver me from seven decades of suppressed wounds. However, when I was suffering in silence, time and chance happens to everyone., When time meets destiny, God will send specialized help. Father knows best. He knew what I needed at the time I needed and in the situation that I needed Him to be my counselor. I learned new sights of God as He reveal new characteristics of Himself to me. I became brand new. I began to believe God again as He showed and revealed Himself real to me in areas that I'd been stuck in for years. Now, I know while suffering in silence because of the myths and stigmas of mental illness, that God never left me nor forsook me.

Whatever I go through, God is able to give me comfort. God always desires a relationship with us. God is revealing Himself to me so I know who I really am and that I am created for a purpose and a reason and will fulfill what He created me to be. He reiterated this to me while revising this book for three years. When I took another look, He was there all the time, but I didn't recognize Him because He came in a different form. God can use a child to reveal His Word and His Will for you and He used my granddaughter, Maya, as we were developing a cover design for this revised version.

Maya, shared this revelation about authenticity. She said, "Grandma you remind me of a person who has been through Kintsugi." Kintsugi is this amazing Japanese art of repairing broken pottery, the practice of "golden repair." When an object is broken, the broken cracks are dusted, brushed, and painted with a special silver, gold or platinum lacquer. All the broken pieces are more beautiful after the reconstruction process, because they are sealed together with gold. Now beautiful scenes of gold glint shine through the cracks of the ceramics, giving it a unique appearance that celebrates and emphasizes its' fractures, cracks and breaks instead of disguising, gluing or hiding them. When the object is finally finished, it is seen as a beautiful unique art form to be put on display, rather than just a broken, repaired, glued together piece of ceramic. Most people are even more beautiful after they have been through a really traumatic experience, if they have taken something away from it and given it to others. I was greatly touched and humbled after she shared her perception of me.

We must learn how to let God break, dust, paint, brush, seal, restore, make and heal us by letting God shine through our cracks. We must benefit from the lessons that He provides for us while walking through some of our really traumatic experiences. Our reconstruction process is necessary in order to make us more beautiful, authentic, valuable and wiser today. God sees all of us, Holy and Whole and will heal our hurts and wounds because He was there all of the time. Everyone experiences Kintsugi, the breakage and the mending process of life. These are all honest parts of our past and should be celebrated and not hidden. They are pieces and parts of who we are. We're more beautiful for having been broken. It's when we show up, cracks and all that we are more Christ like. He will bring a permanent change, cracks and all. Just show up, authentic and humble. Let the Real You Stand Up.

My awareness to newness continued when my daughter, Juanita La Shawn, implemented Warrior Woman Breakthrough To The New You 2018 and asked me to co-chair with her. I was stretched out on God in this new realm of planning and coordinating a conference. This was not an ordinary event, but a purposeful spiritual experience beyond me. God used saved, Holy Ghost-filled Christian Therapists, School Teachers, School Counselors, College Administrators, Prayer Warriors and prayerful friends to download principles for war strategies to regain our mental health and wholeness (Whole, "halo" is holiness).

The move of God was overwhelmingly powerful and purposeful and left us speechless. The power of the conference in the words of Evangelist Regina Barbour was the unity of the body of Christ in action on one accord just like the first church on the day of Pentecost. There were all denominations, races, socio-economic levels, leaders, preachers, battered women, incarcerated, and homeless. The church, was a living organism meeting the needs of the community. We discovered later that the brothers were having a prayer breakfast in the lower level of Grace Evangelistic Church, at the same time. It truly was a family affair. So many committee members were much older and afflicted, but we were stretched beyond our conditions and moved into position. God enabled all of us to function in our purpose, whole.

Everyone was greeted by Warrior Women Elise Andrews, Estelle Boone and the late Carol Christian Brown. Warrior Women Ivy Caddell and Shefronia Candia opened up the hearts of the women and broke up our fallow ground on Friday night in their separate War Rooms after we watched the movie together.

On Saturday morning Warrior Woman Katrina Mitchell led us into the presence of the Lord in worship. Warrior Woman Candy Martin presented her seminar in art, Warrior Woman Dionne Corley warmed our hearts with love and forgiveness, Warrior Woman Regina Barbour placed us in a military counseling session setting and Warrior Woman Martha Taylor took us to the classroom with practical applications. Warrior Woman Anna Baldwin led us in our military march to victory and closed us out in the prophetic. Warrior Woman Monica Armour closed us out understanding that our wounds do heal.

Warrior Woman Wanda Clark set the tone for Saturdays' luncheon when she walked us through the storms of our lives, two by two with an interactive session.

Warrior Woman, Dr. Mary Ann Echols was our keynote luncheon speaker that broke the stigma about therapy for mental health in the church. Shortly after the conference her caseload increased with members from our church and other churches in community. Hallelujah. Special thanks to Elder Lola Slaughter, Sis. Nikki Parchia, Min. Katrina Jones, Sis. Michele Nelms, Sis. Toni Carter, Sis. Thursday Wilson, Sis. Myra Corley, Sis. Alexis Herron, Sis. Maya Bass, Sis. Sabrina Johnson, Sis. Monica Corley, Sis. Tina Robinson, Sis. Cara James, Sis Chyshra Whitfield, The Crew….and many others. Juanita Thompson is also the founder T.H.R.I.V.E Ministries and hosts Little Miss Inner Beauty Pageants and Mother-Daughter Teas annually. Special thanks to Sis. Lynn Phillips, Sis. Lynn Brantley, Sis. Debra Kennedy and Sis. Deborah Carpenter for their untiring love and support. Special thanks to our outstanding Mother-Daughter speakers Regan Nevels and mother and Dr. Angela Thomas, my niece, from Fredericksburg, Virginia.

After the conference it was time to take another X-Ray. I resumed my counseling sessions with Dr. Echols. God was transitioning me out of my emotional reactionary lifestyle into a spiritually responsible lifestyle in the dimension of love.

EXPOSING SPIRITUAL ROOTS

Dr. Echols, a Spirit-filled Clinical Psychologist who God equipped to discern and expose spiritual roots of mental health issues and by-pass years of therapy. I believed in the past as I received secular counseling that I was supposed to learn how to manage my emotions and improve my self-worth. Yet, God provided divine encounters and insight into new dimensions of counseling beyond my past experiences and education.

Dr. Echols stated, "You have are feeling unworthy, unlovable and inadequate. God gave us our emotions because He created us as holistic (body, soul, spirit) beings with emotions, and if we try to shut that part of us down because of painful experiences we become stuck and never fulfill the entire purpose for which we were created. The best way to find true inner healing (finding truth in the inward parts) is to be honest with yourself about what you feel, and then go to God with those issues, seeking answers.

Emotions are God-given, but not God driven. The boundary is peace and when you walk out of it, you cross into and enter the enemies' territory. Unmet emotional needs keep us focused on ourselves and distracted from living life out of purpose. When we have unmet needs, we live in a constant state of neediness because we require acceptance, affirmation, or attention from someone significant just to make it through the day. We continue looking to people to tell us who we are, out of frustration. We continue to venture outside of our own self for our purpose. Until we learn this new way of life of living on purpose instead of striving to meet unmet needs, we will strive for answers.

You must stay in His presence, because in His presence and His Word God will give you the answers that you are seeking. Shift from me, myself and I thinking to being motivated by God's love. Some of your motivations have been an attempt to stop the feelings associated with anxiety. When you move in anxiety you are moving away from God in fear to stop the pain, rather than toward God in love.

She'd continue, "Our feelings were given to us by God and they are not facts, but indicators used to warn us that we need to examine our thoughts. You have a tendency to overthink. But God is teaching you how to live with the pain and suffering when it occurs, not get rid of it. There is a purpose in all of it. Experiences are purposeful for the kingdom ministry. God could stop and block the pain, but when He chooses not to it's because the pain is purposeful, and He has a plan. The struggle is tied to your thoughts, beliefs and perceptions and because of your past you must become vigilant. You under estimate your character and your anointing and presence because you lack the confidence at times.

But you also have humility, and you are in a unique position. Just be aware and stay focused on following God. God gave you unique gifts that are designed to reach the people you are assigned to reach. Fundamentalist have certain traditions and expectations when you are called to preach and teach. Everyone in the audience may not relate to you. You are called to reach certain ones, the ones with mental health issues, who are unconsciously affected by their past deep wounds.

You have a combination of your mixed experiences and His gifts. You are a unique servant in the midst of a place that expects the normal Pentecostal methods and reactions. You are not the norm and because of that, the enemy continues to attack your identity so you can feel less than. You don't even recognize your gifts because you focus on your problems, but walk in the peace.

God is in control and monitors your reactions so it's not fear. True identity in God carries power, love and a sound mind and a presence of a loving God.

Interact without expectations, be humble, prefer your brother or sister and just be, don't feel rejected. Let the free flow of the truth and power of God shine through you, no matter what. Your intention shouldn't be to offend anybody, but possess a motive pure to love from the spirit. Anxiety coupled with the fear of being rejected is fleshly and carnal living. There is a natural reality and a spiritual reality which is to mold you into the image of Christ. Be still and wait on God.

Speak to the anxiety which is the root of confusion and lack of confidence. Anxiety wants you to react right away, but get away. Social anxiety wants you to withdraw or attack. Anxiety compels you to defend, protect, withdraw.... (Evang. Carmella Hill would say flight, freeze or fight.) Peace requires that the first action is to pray. Whenever the emotion crops its head, stop and pray, don't do anything else.

Your motive is purest when you intend to follow God. Be obedient to God and serve God. Go where He leads you and not where anxiety drives you. When flesh tries to control you to block the pain so you won't hurt, follow Jesus by His example of standing with His wounds. He was wounded and He's still standing which is His response to pain. Your goal is to keep reaffirming your identity, grace and power in His presence and live in the moment, standing in peace. You must be motivated in love to live in peace. Your responsibility is to surrender, obey and submit (S.O.S) to remain in peace, when you step over boundaries you will know it because you will step out of peace into anxiety. Stay in peace."

When Dr. Echols dealt with rebuilding and recovering from broken relationships she taught me the principle SOS, surrender, obey and submit as a strategy for emotional healing.

"You have been trying to submit before you surrender. SURRENDER. OBEY SUBMIT (S.O.S.). There is such a difference between submission and surrender we often use the terms interchangeably."

SURRENDER: "Whatever the emotional, mental and physical reaction on the inside is, open up and let it go, hand it over to God."

Dr. Harry Tiebout says "The emotional state of surrender is a state in which there is a persisting capacity to accept reality. It is a state that is really positive and creative. As Christians, there is a call to surrender to the Holy Spirit. Philippians 3:21 "Who, by the power that enables him to bring everything under his control, will transform our lowly bodies so that they will be like His glorious body."

Followers of Jesus are called to a full surrender where we put up no residual battle once we have accepted the reality of the Holy Spirit's control. We still have areas where we have submitted, but not surrendered all. There remains this pull and tension to not accept all the realities of a life controlled and led by God.

Surrender means that a believer completely gives up his own will and subjects his thoughts, ideas, and deeds to the will and teachings of Jesus Christ. Surrender is the willful acceptance and yielding to a dominating force and their will. Surrender means to stop fighting and resisting someone. Surrender is characterized with struggle. We surrender when we are in love. We are willing to do what God desires. This helps overcoming stumbling blocks to belief.

Obedience: "Do whatever He tells you to do immediately whether you feel it or not." A mentally healthy person is one who has God-worth and Godly-love. They love themselves, and obey the two commandments with promise in St. Matthew 22:37-39, "Love the Lord… love thy neighbor as thyself." There is a power in loving yourself.

The performance of what is required by authority or abstaining from what is prohibited. Obedience is voluntary or involuntary, but voluntary obedience is acceptable by God. Obedience is yielding compliance with commands, orders or injunctions performing what is required, or abstaining from what is forbidden. We are obedient when we obey His Word from the heart otherwise we're just following rules.

What He places in our hearts must be spoken and birth and participate with Him.

SUBMIT: "When pressure comes from the outside of you, don't struggle with people, emotions, verbal abuse or people lying on you. There is a resolve or a pre-work inside of you where the spirit must say yes. Whatever is required of you and you remain postured where you expect God to move."

Submission is defined as the quality or condition of being submissive, obedient, meek, and resigned. Submit to the will of God, even when you feel broken because God's got it. God is glorified in brokenness because your total dependence is on Him.

She continues, **"Broken to Be Made Whole is a fundamental truth and is based upon perception. God has been breaking off any perceived strengths in your own eyes and causing you to see yourself in His eyes, strong in Him. It is the ready recognition of a higher authority. There is no resistance. There is meekness and obedience. Submission is characterized with peace.**

When you communicate and relate to others, you will experience better relationships when you do conflict resolution. Ask yourselves the following questions.

1. Did this individual ask me for help or do I need to listen and support? Most of the time most people need a listening ear rather than advice. We have a tendency as loved ones to rescue and as leaders to preach and teach.
2. Are my emotions in check? Because when you're trying to help people your issues may get mixed up with theirs if you're not in touch with your own emotions.
3. Is there a message that God through the Holy Ghost wants me to communicate to others? The most powerful is not emotional, but Spiritual communication expressed with grace and love.
4. Can I speak in love and not judgment? When boundaries are enmeshed or you are taking on the responsibility of another with the intention of protecting others from hurting, it's hard to separate facts from feelings.

When we approach counseling with our past experiences the fallacy as helpers, is that we confuse help with the outcome. We are supposed to provide the help, but we cannot be responsible for the outcome. We plant the seeds. However, if we have a need for validation, and we expect appreciation for the outcome, that's emotional when we make it about ourselves. It's all about God.

Many times the counsel can be judgmental and then you feel that you have to defend yourself against the attack. God says when they slap you on one cheek, turn the other cheek. Don't waste time defending yourself, because we don't answer to anybody but God. When we spend time trying to defend and justify it's a distraction that wastes good time and energy. Let God fight our battles.

Ask God to bring life when we interact with people that we love. When we're patient He'll bring truth to us.

The best way to deal with our emotions is to:

1. Catch It (them) when we are upset and angry and crossing boundaries we walked away from peace. Return back to peace.
2. Check It- Am I saying it in love or judgment. Truth or fear.
3. Change It- Change it to reflect love and not anger, spiritual and not emotional.
4. That's the only way seeds grow, with light and water. So stop planting a seed into the lives of others and stomp on it. We plant good seeds, then we stomp on it, jump up and down on it and beat and the ground then try to make it grow ourselves before our eyes demanding fruit."

God revealed that I was raped forty-five years ago and buried the shame, hurt and fear underneath the anger. I internalized the feelings of betrayal and guilt for years and held them in my "gut" which resulted in many hospitalizations for severe constipation. I asked Dr. Echols, "Why can't I seem to heal from this broken heart?"

Her response, "Anxiety keeps resurfacing because it's triggered by wounds and hurts that happened in the past. The challenge is how you deal with the anxiety when it comes. When your emotions are triggered, instead of taking the truth of God's Word, you try to control your emotions by answering with anxiety. Anxiety's response is too quick, overdone and last too long. It interferes with your ability to function and the enemy gets a foothold in your thoughts. It becomes a stronghold that causes you to oppose the will of God. Then you resort back to self-doubt and conclude that you don't have enough faith.

But remember the 3 F's.

1. **FEELINGS** – Identify the fear or hurt, don't hide behind the anger but give them to God. Don't Stuff it or suppress it into your body. Release them.
2. **FACTS** - What does God say? What does the Spirit, say?
3. **FAITH** – Step out in faith to confront fear. Stop the fear in its tracks with Faith in God's Word.

Learn how to integrate faith with everyday living. Love conquers all fear and a sound mind places God in charge and He will led and guide you into all truth. The truth will weaken and dissipate all of the lies that you have believed about yourself. You are saved, but choose different outcomes.

1. You walk as a believing Christian in your freedom and wholeness as long as your faith is activated. You are a believer and you will know it because you will have more confidence, peace and love.
2. When you choose to walk by your feelings and emotions and not by faith, you are an unbelieving Christian, and walk in confusion, controlling behaviors and unrest motivated by the lies that you believe. Our failures are not based on what others did or didn't do. But it's how we react. **Brokenness is not the problem, but what we do with it."**

God is in control and monitors your reactions so it's not fear. True identity in God carries power, love and a sound mind and a presence of a loving God. Interact without expectations, be humble prefer your brother or sister just be and don't feel rejected. But let the free flow of the truth and power of God shine through you, no matter what. Your intention shouldn't be to offend anybody, but a motive pure from the spirit, not from the flesh which is anxiety coupled with the fear of being rejected. There is a natural reality and a spiritual reality which is to mold you into the image of Christ. Be still and wait on God. Speak to the anxiety which is the root of confusion and lack of confidence. Anxiety wants you to react right away, but get away, be still and know God. Social anxiety wants you to withdraw or attack. Anxiety compels you to defend, protect, withdraw.... (Evangelist Carmella Hill would say flight, freeze or fight.) Peace requires that the first action is to pray.

Whenever the emotion crops its head, stop and pray, don't do anything else. Your motive is purest when you intend to follow God. Be obedient to God and serve God. Go where He leads you and not where anxiety drives you. When flesh tries to control you, block the pain so you won't hurt, but follow Jesus by the example of Him standing with His wounds. I was wounded and I'm still standing is His response to pain. Your goal is to keep reaffirming your identity, grace and power in His presence and live in the moment standing in peace. Your responsibility is to surrender, obey and submit (S.O.S) to remain in peace, you will

In this new dimension I awoke out of sleep and got to know myself better, more fully and in a new way. I was awakening to wholeness because it is the awakening of my heart, to the unlimited possibilities of my spiritual nature that caused me to come alive again. When I understand that emotions were not my friend, but a foe, I began to use them as indicators to trace the root of the wound and transform me, heal me, and restore strength and energy. God restored my stamina, joy and desire to be a servant leader once again.

While moving into my new normal God called other men and women were called alongside to help in the ministry of Mental Health for the church. By now God revealed Himself as He raised up intercessors throughout the neighboring counties, cities and states, as well as the Mahoning Valley. One life coach, at the best kept secret Inner Healing day spas would often instruct me to be still and discern which tree am I standing at today, the tree of life or the tree of good and evil?

In April 2019 Luther and I attended a Be In Health, Overcomer's Weekend Conference. Real Solutions in Cincinnati, Ohio, because I was curious about the strategies of Dr. Henry Wright ministry for my broken hearts. The late, Dr. Henry Wright was the visionary of Be In Health and the author of - A More Excellent Way, Exposing the Spiritual Roots of Disease and many other books and tools. God transformed his life from an abusive childhood while suffering at the hand of a father who was a minister, into a lifetime of a ministry of exposing spiritual, mental and emotional blockages to enable healing and wholeness. His testimony motivated me to continue to minister in holistic healing. **He exposed how the spiritual roots of an unloving spirit and the effects of a broken heart profoundly impacted my life. I thank my friend Regina Barbour for diligently seeking God on my behalf and gifting me the book, A More Excellent Way,**

Be in Health. Col 2:1-10 states that thankfulness and gratefulness is a great weapon against mental illness.

I learned a valuable key principle that God revealed at the conference in Timothy 2:24-26. It states, "As a servant of the Lord Jesus Christ, we are to be kind to everyone. The Lord is kind and he expects the same from His servants. Kindness is the part the fruit of the spirit that should be true of every servant of Christ."

During our Thanksgiving service in 2019, Elder Kent Barnes preached, Guardians of Gratitude, a prolific message emphasizing the importance of how gratitude will move you from your disabled condition to your ability to function in God and in this Next move of God, He will use us. Hum, from disabled condition to my ability to function in God? Yes!

Now I have a better understanding of the revelation my spiritual son, Bishop Willie Thornton, ministered when he said, "Mom, you are going to uproot and tear down, destroy and overthrow, build and plant in your new season."

My spiritual son, Elder Joseph Bowers would download encouragement, prophecies and visions regarding the direction that God has for me and rehearse "There is purpose in your pain, Mom. Just give the Lord clean hands."

Pastor and Evang. Tyson have been encouraging us, as senior citizens to continue to see our worth and value beyond our retirement years. We can reach out and minister to the broken and bullied population within our community. I admire the work that Deacon Wilbur and Sister Linda Drayton do within the community with the youth and the seniors within the church and began to embrace the message from our leadership.

Simultaneously, Mt. Calvary began a month of Mental Health in the Church and continued with the series exiting 2019 entering into 2020, ALMOST THERE. The entire church took X-Rays or Self-Examination Inventories. Where Am I?

1. Spiritually
2. Emotionally
3. Physically
4. Intellectually
5. Vocationally
6. Relationally
7. Financially

God revealed to me that the new thoughts of my husband and I were elated when both Pastor Tyson and First Lady Tyson presented the segment on Emotional well-being. Excerpts from the teaching are:

II Corinthians 13:5, "Examine yourselves, whether ye be in the faith; prove your own selves." Having and expressing our emotions does not mean we are unspiritual; it means we are human. Genesis 1:31 .... we are good and very good. A denial of our humanity is a rejection of God's divinity.

Feeling = Sympatheo means to be affected. Faith is not what I feel. Faith is who I know and what I believe. Prayer won't stop you from having feelings, but it will prevent your feelings from compromising your faith.

Acceptance is the answer to all of my problems today. When I am disturbed it is because I find some person, place, thing, or situation some fact of my life unacceptable to me, and I can find no serenity until I accept that person, place or thing or situation as being exactly the way it is supposed to be at this moment. Recovery. I need to concentrate not so much on what needs to be changed in the world as what needs to be changed in me and in my attitudes.

Recovery from anything involves overcoming a disease of the attitudes. We get in our own way when we choose to blame others, wallow in self-pity, or focus our energy on what we cannot do. This has the net effect of making us stressed out, depressed, and anxious. All of that energy wasted just to avoid the daunting possibility of change. Our emotions respond to a signal the mind sends. You determine your physical man by choice of thoughts you hold and believe. Your emotions, regardless of the nature, are the product of your thoughts. Change your thinking and you will change your emotions. Proverbs 15:23 A man hath joy by the answer of his mouth; and a word spoken in due season, how good is it. **It is not what happens to you that determines your happiness, it's your answer to what happens to you that determines your happiness."**

During the pandemic God the new thoughts and ideas are based upon responding to God's I Love You's in an attempt to get our attention. We haven't focused and responded because the voice of God and the sounds from Heaven, are different and better what we've been use to in the past. He's chastening us and correcting us because He simply wants the best for us. Now is the time to make the changes. If not now then when? God continued to arrange a series of divine set-ups during the Covid 19 coronavirus pandemic when social media exposed us to consistent dynamic impactful ministries that I enjoyed them as an observer.

These encounters with God came when I least expected them. The shift came as God gently transitioned me into my Next, during the summer months of July, August and September, 2020. When I taught Inner Healing in some churches for twenty years, it involved teaching the principles of prayer, forgiveness, repentance, rejecting lies and replacing them with truth and processing painful memories to bring emotional and spiritual healing and laying hands on them. Now what? Social media seemed challenging for me because I never used it.

I was intimidated when Sister Dedra Preston extended an invitation to me to participate on a panel on social media on behalf of the West Virginia - East Tennessee Council. My assignment was my testimony regarding their theme, Pursuing A Victorious Life Through Good Mental Health. I hadn't ministered for ten or twelve years and wasn't use to technology. Dr. Mary Ann Echols encouraged me to accept the challenge when she said, "Do it for God. Someone needs to hear your testimony as an overcomer." God used Dr. Marion Wright, a psychiatrist and Evangelist Paulette Foster, a clinical therapist and myself as a team. We fulfilled our assignment to bring Mental Health Awareness as Christians regarding Trauma, ADHD and Bipolar-Depression. We also dispelled church stigmas and myths regarding counseling. Mental illness is not a sign of a lack of faith and should no longer be considered a demon that people should be delivered from or exorcized.

Immediately, Evangelist Ivy Caddell extended an invitation to participate on her Healing School phone conference as a guest for two weeks following Evangelist Ruby Bostic-Forgiveness, Elder Ralph Johnson- The Importance of Water and preceding Evangelist Shefronia Candia- Cleansing Our Colon and others speakers on Raw Foods and Essential Oils. Yes, my topic was Mental Health Wellness. God's anointing rode on the vision He'd given me of a lion that had his mouth on my throat to prevent me from speaking and just as he went to devour and bite my jugular vein, the anointing of God flung the lion off my neck and I was free. The yoke of fear and bondage from the reoccurring memory of my father's hand around my mother's neck to silence her was destroyed. Isaiah 10:27 states, "And it shall come to pass in that day, that his burden shall be taken from off thy shoulder, and his yoke shall be destroyed because of the anointing."

Before I completed the assignment my sister, Denise, extended an invitation to participate on a panel on Colorism hosted by Dr. Sabrina Black, psychologist and co-hosted by my sister, Evangelist Denise Smith, a licensed counselor. There were between twelve and sixteen powerful women weekly who were psychologists, therapists, attorneys, a mother of eleven daughters, housewives, rap artists, filmmakers, pastors, authors, businesswomen, higher education educators and some of the panelists' mothers. There was generational synergy that spanned at least five generations. I declined the invitation mainly because I'd never heard of Colorism, or so I thought. However, it became apparent that I was broken by colorism most of my life. These great women from various denominations shared their testimonies every Monday for three weeks during August 2020. Early Tuesday morning, August 22, 2020, I experienced a divine encounter. God Himself, (His presence) illuminated our bedroom, wrapped His arms around me and took me back to childhood pains and removed every name that I'd been called, healed every rejection, every negative experience, the hurts, the wounds and took the pain out of the memory. I hollered, screamed, wept, and I rolled as I woke my husband, Luther, out of his sleep. He began to pray and participate with God. It was a divine intervention that I will never forget. We had an old fashioned deliverance service in the bedroom. I was able to release my pain, sorrow, humiliation regarding the effects of Colorism (a form of racial discrimination and prejudice against individuals typically individuals who are darker, and in some instances lighter skin within the same race and ethnic group or color struck). The emotional bondage that subconsciously and unconsciously invaded my life was over. The sexual molestations and rape was healed. The effects from bullying was over. The pain of the memory rejection was gone. I was no longer angry. God revealed the hidden shame and guilt from feeling I'll never measure up or I'm not good enough was a lifetime preparation for a latter day ministry of restoration and reconciliation for the broken hearted. Wow, I was trying to "fit in" with the other ministers and He never called me to fit in.

As I shared the deliverance with my sister, I accepted the offer to appear on their panel as a guest to render a sincere expression of gratitude and thanks. I thanked them for modeling their authenticity, genuineness, and rawness. They were supportive and a safe place to share.

They ushered me into my Next assignment which is to uproot and pull down strongholds with a testimony, not always the traditional preaching and teaching.

Risking, sharing and telling our stories is one very important component in Inner Healing. When we risk, we expose ourselves. We take a chance and become vulnerable and either become accepted or rejected by taking a chance and sharing our story. When we hold our feelings, thoughts and concerns in, we become stifled and we store negative energy that eventual implodes within or manifest in an unhealthy manner, physically, emotionally, or mentally. Ministering as an overcomer and risk sharing my testimony is serving the body of Christ. Discovering, feeling, exposing, and releasing opens doors to the power of God which will cause us to live a successful, fruitful, peaceful and joyous life in Christ Jesus.

When God filled my mouth with truths and anointed utterances, I was invited to participate during the last two weeks of an extension. During the last session in September, powerful new words and sounds of instruction flowed emphatically out of my mouth, Find It, Face IT, Let God Fix It. I was elated because this wisdom came from my spirit from a download during several of my counseling sessions with Dr. Echols. I haven't been the same. God literally broke me for the last time in several areas. I'm now a willing vessel to minister as I stay in my lane and fulfill the call to minister healing to the specific audience that I'm assigned to.

Excited to share my victory with Dr. Echols and how God thundered the healing words, Find It, Face it, and Let God Fix It we reviewed the impact of the entire experience. Her session notes were life changing.

She summarized, 'The truths that you've learned and applied have set you free. The reality is when you receive the truth, apply the truth of what God gave you, you now must give back because you have been freed to deliver God's message to others. St. John 8:32, "And ye shall know the truth, and the truth shall set you free." The enemy masks at distorting reality but you must move in spirituality.

Don't seek for affirmation in wrong places of emotions. We feel it's ideal to hide from emotional disasters and operate in delusions and believe that I'm okay. Psalms 51:6 says God doesn't work like that so we must open the door of our accusers and stop running from emotions that distort the truth and believe lies. Hurt and anxiety reactions are exploits that are inferior thinking and inadequate responses. Our thinking regarding suffering weakens us in the natural, but allows God to strengthen us spiritually for His purposes of lifting us, and revealing Himself and His character. Suffering has always been part of Gods plan. Suffering has value and purpose.

If God loves me, why does He allow the suffering? He already knows bad things that happen are controlled by the devil. When we serve God there's a freedom and a peace when we believe that God turns the evil and hurt to His glory and yields a better end. There's no shame in pain and suffering, but we must believe there's a purpose in it or we'll get mad and remain angry.

1. FIND IT- Comes by revelation as God speaks conviction in our spirit and redirects and corrects us. She uses the example when she initially confronted me on my perception of love."

   "I thought I was being loving, but the reality was an inaccurate understanding of who I was. I made a 360 degree full turn and allowed God to teach me about His love.

   I assumed that loving and being loved were the same. I truly believed when people are loved, we would become whole. But, being loved doesn't always enable us to become whole, if we never learned how to love. Love from others cannot make us worthy, if we never learned how to love ourselves. Love cannot fill our void of what we feel is missing in us. It cannot erase what is faulty. Or mend what is broken. Or hide what we do not want to be seen. Love is not a stamp of approval, of the knight or knightess and shining armors coming to our rescue in marriage or companionship believing once we belonged to someone, our lives would have purpose. Love cannot do for us what we must learn to receive for ourselves. Love is not defensive.

   Love enhances what we've already received from God and given to ourselves. The truth is being a whole person enables us to love. Love is a skill that needs to be learned. Love is to have the willingness to interpret someone's not so appealing behavior in order to find reasons to administer charity and generosity and pray for them.

   We are spiritual beings experiencing human love with love/hate tendencies loving and hating the same person until we mature. Maturity teaches us that anyone we love will disappoint us and that there are no heroes to be admired because eventually those closest to us or those that we admire will either learn to tolerate our weakness in order to continue to love us or leave us.

When marriages are reciprocal with a genuine give and take and actually "becoming one", it's a beautiful experience, well beyond the level of "sex" only, when it's done according to God's plan. No one else can make you happy nor do for you what you must learn to do for yourself.

Who God made me to be was important, because He uses ordinary people, and I didn't have to be perfect to be loved. He saved me and used me broken, to work in the ministry. I was whole because He created me whole, and whatever damage I did to myself was repairable in the Master's Hands alone. In His eyesight I've always been perfectly whole." I was learning how to celebrate the love that God gave me.

2. "FACE IT- Accept how you played a part from start to end in your own misery and the emotional way you reacted." Slow down and pray, then respond based on God's Words of mercy, grace and truth."

   Love is not defensive. The more defensive and controlling a person is the less worth and value they possess. Pay attention when you are judgmental, but respond in a non-judgmental way. Our judgment in the natural is flawed and unkind because in our flesh we react to one another based on our feelings from the experience. God's purpose is greater than our emotions.

3. "LET GOD FIX IT- Cast your cares upon Him. Vengeance is mine saith the Lord. Be still and know that I am God. Fix our eyes upon Jesus. Shut your mouth, God has gone before you to win the battle. You are stronger than you think."

   I received my breakthrough to the new me, a new way of life after a series of crisis, challenges, tests, trials, tribulations, Bible classes, messages, prayer lines, zooms and counseling sessions. The in house conventions, conferences, revivals, retreats prayer breakfasts and fellowships were canceled by God. Our new normal was based on revelations gleaned on social media. I appreciate the revelation shared regarding Isaiah 65:8, "Thus saith the Lord, as the new wine is found in the cluster, and one saith, Destroy it not for a blessing is in it; so will I do for my servants sakes, that I may not destroy them all." This powerful woman of God shared, **"There is new wine in the cluster."** Here's hope for everyone that suffered in silence with mental health issues or have loved ones that they support.

There is a process in becoming new. The process of brokenness, restoration, transformation and wholeness is cyclical. Whenever God is revealing or doing a new thing, there will always be an unlayering of something old to discover and uncover something new. Isaiah 43:19 states, "Behold, (be alert, be present look, look again, change your perception), I will do a new thing; now it shall spring forth; shall ye not know (perceive) it?" I will even make a way in the wilderness, and rivers in the desert. God truly made my crooking thinking straight, the key to many mental health issues, not all, but many.

When God changed my perception (the way I see) to His Reality (the way God sees) brokenness, instantly a light bulb came on, which was a revelatory moment that began to change my perception of who I am in Him. Remember, a broken spirit makes a person a joy to be around. He has a tenderness in manner, a gratitude for what others do, a humility about himself, and a gentleness in relating to others who have faults. God is nigh to the broken and God heals the broken in heart because He ministers inner healing and truth on the inward parts. He offered transforming the hidden places within.

God Wants Us Whole

A whole person is one who has worth and love based upon God's principles (unconditional, divine love) and not the principalities (conditional, human love) of the world. Instead of the emphasis being on self-worth and self-image I shifted to knowing God-worth and a Godly-image.

Until I learned to love God, then myself, then and only then will I really know how to allow God to love others through me. I would always experience stress related-illnesses. When I would continue to walk in the correct interpretation of the commandments I would thrive. At times, it's been difficult to break up the fallow, hardened, irrational Belief-Systems, those strongholds, that seem immovable. Apostle Paul taught us that we must press forward to learn to live from the "inside out" rather than from the outside in. Our true source of love comes from the power, love and sound mind residing on the inside of us and learning how to tap into that power within.

Before I could give or receive love I had to learn how to forgive. Forgiveness is the final form of love. Forgiveness is a key principle for success, happiness, joy, restoration and healing. Forgiveness teaches you to give the love back to yourself that you forfeited when you held others hostage and failed to let go of their offenses. Forgiveness increases your love bank account and unforgiveness leaves deficits, withdrawals and negative balances in your bank account. Forgiveness literally expedites and speeds up our spiritual, mental, emotional, social, financial, relational and physical healings. Forgiveness ushers us into wholeness.

What does wholeness look like? What does wholeness sound like? The word whole or "hale is connected with the word heal. The quality of or state of being without limitations, restrictions, distractions and wantonness. Wholeness is where your heart must be made whole in its desire towards God, yet broken for its sin. Wholeness is found in the core of our being, the pure heart that is evidenced by the ability to love and live in peace. Wholeness is holiness living in the unconditional, divine love of God being our authentic selves, by transformation, returning to our state of being as complete and harmoniously whole. A whole person rests in whose they are, who they are and where they are in life, while seeking personal growth for the benefit of self and others. They are able to see their wounds and not hide them nor condemn themselves for having them. They are able to embrace themselves with acceptance and grace.

Begin to know yourself by spending quality time with yourself. Know when God has reframed your mind and put the pieces back together again. It is a matter of timing. You can be new and don't realize it or you can think that you are and you're not quite there yet.

Wholeness is actually the end result of voluntary brokenness. Brokenness is recognized as God's requirement for human usefulness. Brokenness is also perceived as God's vehicles of transportation that drives us to our destiny.

Whole defined in Colossians 2:10 states, "And ye are complete in him, which is the head of all principality and power. "Wholeness is being complete where there is nothing you are wanting or nothing you are missing. We are completely whole in Him.

In the Young's Literal Translation it states, "And ye are made full, who is the head of all principality and authority." There is no principality, power, ruler of darkness of this world, or spiritual wickedness in high places that can prevail against us.

A Biblical definition means the state of being perfectly balanced and well in spirit, body and soul (mind, will and emotions). Wholeness is "halo" which means holy or wholly. When a person is saved they are delivered from their sins and eternal separation from God and can become whole or holy.

Salvation is the first step toward regaining complete wholeness. Our spirits become fully alive, (regenerated) and we are completely alive and well in our spirit. We are sanctified from a spiritual perspective.

In Colossians 3, God valued me setting my affections on Him in an intimate relationship and being complete in Him. He valued the development of the fruit of the spirit in Galatians 5. He valued the weapons of His spiritual warfare of prayer and fasting in Ephesians 6. He valued His Name, His Word, His Blood, the Blood of Jesus. He loves to be praised and worshipped. He values those individuals who love and respect His children, His prized creation and those who chose to become His sons (daughters).

The Blood of Jesus overcomes and heals every circumstance and situation. The Word of God divides the soul from the spirit, releasing the spirit to become the dominate force in our lives and not our emotions and five senses.

In retrospect looking back twenty eight years ago, when I was totally surrendered to God and walked in the newness of light, He did some amazing ministry through me. You see, setting my affections on things above have been more valuable than impressing people, traveling to places and accumulating things.

It was Jesus, not a car, money, fame, prestige, power, a husband, friends, degrees, etc. that was there with my only sister, on the faithful day of December 8, 1992. I used the weapons of intercessory prayer, praise and worship all day. I was troubled in my spirit and didn't understand why. When I shared with my friend, Evangelist Regina Hall-Barbour, she discerned that God was nudging, prompting and urging me to draw nigh unto Him. For several hours I laid prostrate on my face worshipping and praising God, then interceding in prayer and tears. I was travailing, but didn't know why. After five hours, God said,

"I want you to praise me for every miracle." I began to praise him for miracles in the Bible and He said, "No, praise me for healing your friend, Delbert Brogdon when he was burned in a fire at work and I restored the skin on his face like a baby's skin." I continued to praise

Him for several others. Now I understood what Elder Ross taught us regarding immediate obedience to prayer will save someone's life. When we feel God tugging at our hearts to pray, stop whatever you're doing, roll out of the bed or drop to your knees, and hit the floor praying no matter what, you may be used by God to save someone's life.

Pastor Tyson recently taught us about the power of Proactive Prayer vs Reactive Prayer and in retrospect this is what I experienced on this faithful day twenty-eight years ago. God had me pray a proactive prayer, getting ahead of the situation rather than react once the incident occurred.

In the midst of intercessory prayer and worship, Luther received a phone call from my sister in-love, Chally, at that time, stating that my sister, Denise, had been shot. Initially, I panicked and was anxious, but within seconds, God said, "Remember that list of miracles I told you to praise me for? You can add your sister, Denise, to the list." Glory!

She was a Detroit probation officer who had just remanded one of her probationers back to prison for a probation violation. Her probationer hired a hitman and put a contract out for her to be killed. When the hitman approached her in front of our parents' home, on Sorrento, even though she usually carries a gun, the only weapon she used was the authority, in The Blood of Jesus, that saved her life. When she called on Jesus name, and said, "Jesus, Jesus, Jesus", her account is that the hitman pointed the gun at her heart, chest and upper body, and it seemed as though she tripped, but an Angel gently placed her on the ground on her back.

Instead of blowing holes in her physical heart, he shot her 5 times with a 9 millimeter gun in her stomach and groin. It was The Blood of Jesus that covered and healed her body. When my pastor, the late Bishop N.L.Wagner flew me home, it was seriously just in the nick of time. The hospital wasn't allowing anymore visitors in my sisters' room because she needed her rest to live. However, God prevailed and we were able to worship together as we sang the blood songs even with the tube in her mouth.

Did she have a broken heart, holes, and emotional wounds? Yes! Did the family grieve, even though a few of us were saved? Yes! Did we understand? No! Did we question God and ask Him Why? Yes! However, the moment my sister asked me to join her and others to pray, intercede and ask God to reveal and prosecute the perpetrators, my focus shifted beyond my emotions into seeking mercy and justice. God Did it.

I had to shift into being proactive in praise and worship. Glory be to God, within six months, the hitman came to the probation office and asked so many questions, until he may as well turned himself in. He was arrested as a suspect, tried, convicted, sentenced and received two life sentences. He admitted his guilt, but refused to reveal the name of the person that hired him. The person who hired him was released from prison and was murdered a few years later. We had to learn to trust God even in the midst of a trauma. Vengeance is mine saith the Lord, even in cold cases with seemingly no closure, God'got it!

Did The Lord, God Our Savior, Jesus Christ receive all of the Glory as she wrote the account in her book, Back From Sanity's Edge? Yes! Denise Smith is a living testimony twenty-eight years later, as she states as Apostle Paul wrote in, Romans 8:28: "And we know that all things work together for good to them that love God, to them who are the called according to his purpose." You can't quit God when life happens. Life happens and it does hurt. As Christians we can never pray, fast, read the Bible, give and do good things to prevent bad things from happening. But when they do, we can use the things of the spirit to walk us through the hurt, brokenness, grief and the pain. Pain is inevitable, but misery is optional.

We can live whole lives in a broken world when we live our lives with purpose and intention.

We ARE BROKEN TO BE MADE WHOLE! There are many who have courageously picked up the pieces of their shattered lives like my sister and have received break throughs to new lives.

God has an expected end with us in mind between starting broken and ending whole. God states there is a process to receiving the promises, but He has to prepare us by using the pieces of our lives that we perceived as mistakes in the past. He wants us to **recognize** that this was really only part of the learning process. God sends us into an arena where He creates. God has gone into our lives and created whatever He desired for us to experience in dysfunctional relationships. He allowed them to be created in order to crack our egg at the right time, to get our yolk out of us, the core of our very being and essence.

Even though He cracked our egg, He wants us to take the **responsibility** to get rid of all those shells lying around by admitting their there and bringing the pieces to Him. Shells are not part of the recipe for an expected end of a cake. We get hung up on getting the broken pieces of our shells, but those breaks that violated and fragmented us when we bite into the cake don't belong in the end product, the cake.

God does reveal how to get the fun out of dys**fun**ction. Many times when we are ready to eat God's word, we bite into the shell of a memory and the bite triggers our past lives. It's at this time that we must learn how to **repent** for our generational iniquities of the past to break that effect on future generation. We were broken to be pliable enough to get in God's mix, as children we are created very resilient and **restored** back to God's original purpose. But this childish egg must be broken, runny, and must have the form and consistency that was housed in the egg. God could not make us into a cake without the egg yolk, and he refuses to leave us in the old state, but **renews** us so we can be transformed by our new minds.

Now that we have strength and a **resolve, we** can and will deposit light in those dark areas of our lives that we experienced. Everyone in life and every experience, the good, the bad and the ugly, was an instrument to prepare us to receive the promises embodied in Him. God is watching over us and we won't get burned in the fiery furnaces of making, shaping and molding on the potter's wheel. We will get dizzy and spin a bit but do not focus on the negatives, but the blessings in the lessons.

In a new place, with new hopes and dreams the fulfillment of the internal healings and promises required breaking at a new level for entrance into new dimensions to **reinvent** ourselves in His image.

When we reflect back and secured old promises that hadn't manifest yet, we must speak life and resurrection power into the promises and commanded they LIVE. The **resolve** that God gives us in our spirit is incredible and this enemy (in-a-me) we will not see anymore.

I have been **reinventing** myself ever before and since the pandemic in quiet and solitude. The spirit of fear will leave for a season and return back to see if I am still standing. The reality with fear is that fear is part of an ungodly trinity according to our Pastor C. Shawn Tyson and I yield and practice my S.O.S, (surrender, obey and submit) daily.

This season is an opportunity and a call to take the Seventh step to reinvent ourselves. The definition of the word reinvent means to produce something new that is based on something that already exists or to remake or make over, as in a different form. Some methods of ministries have changed, but my assignment to minister to the broken hearted remains the same with an addition to the assignment. I learned to have empathy for myself. Today God has elevated me to a new dimension of revelation knowledge and wisdom beyond my formal education in school counseling. He's training me in the realm of deliverance by pulling down spiritual roots. I'm learning to discern spiritual roots much better and He's directing me daily. I'm excited about this breakthrough into a new dimension. I'm grateful that God is my help and my strength. I love Him.

CONCLUSION

Today, the church, modern health care workers and counselors are realizing the need to care for the whole person, body, soul and spirit. Mental Health care workers and pastors are discovering the tremendous benefits of spirit-mind-body connections that support an abundant life. Several athletes, actors and actresses are using their celebrity status to garner the attention of Congress. Taraji P. Henson, Jennifer Lewis, Prince Harry, Mariah Carey, Dwayne "The Rock" Johnson and so many celebrities are bringing valuable awareness to the importance of Mental Health.

Former First Lady, Michelle Obama shared recently on her podcast she was suffering from low-grade depression which she attributes to coronavirus quarantine, the mental health toll of racism in addition to political issues. She suggested staying connected to loved ones and taking a social media break which helps her get out of a bad place. This is the season that God is using a diversity of people to address Mental Health issues.

In this season, God is looking for broken vessels to bless for their faith and hardships by making up for their losses and giving them more than they had previously. There is a special blessing for those who intercede as what the Bible calls, "gap dwellers" who minister to others through their season of affliction. Psalms 34:18-19, states: "The Lord is nigh unto them that are of a broken heart and a contrite spirit. Many are the afflictions of the righteous, but the Lord delivereth him out of them all."

Psalms 34:18 God is kin to us when we are barely standing on our own two feet like the images of the essential workers, the health care professionals and hospital staff workers seen and unseen. The Lord is kin to those who have grown weary. Psalms 34:19. Only God can heal our broken hearts and the unbearable losses we don't yet understand.

But we must take responsibility for our wounded spirits and ask God for strength and He will grant it to you.

A broken heart is intensely sad and sorrowful and it seems as though it will never go away.

Time will help, but God heals the heart that is broken from the excruciating pain. Things that broke our hearts are usually the human experience in relationships that are outside of us and out of our control. When that happens God is right there. I leave you with the eight steps that God used to heal me and pray that it heals you.

St. John 3:16 For God so loved the world, that he gave his only begotten Son, that whosoever believeth in him should not perish, but have everlasting life.

8 Steps to Wholeness

1. **Recognize** no one is designed to live with their background holding their back to the ground. Get up, accept your purpose and identity in Christ Jesus.
2. **Be Responsible (response-able)** for your own needs and happiness using boundaries. Boundaries will cause you to return back to the authentic and original person that God created you to be.
3. **Repent** from dead works which releases you from repressed, suppressed, stuffed emotions and spiritual strongholds that opened illegal doors for the enemy. Repentance opens the doors to change your perception towards godly, scriptural, holy things.
4. **Be restored**. Restoration heals your broken heart and damaged emotions from broken relationships and allows you to be healed beyond measure, greater than your condition before salvation. Forgive!
5. **Be renewed**. Renewing your mind corrects your thinking and your choices. When you change your thoughts, you make healthy choices and God makes the changes.
6. **Be resolute**. Resolve to love unconditionally because you can depend on the immutable, veracity of God's promises. Psalms 147:3, "He healeth the broken in heart and bindeth up their wounds."
7. **Request a miracle** in your memory and healing in your brain. Prayer is vital to the process.
8. **Reinvent yourself by celebrating the love that God has given to you.** Love is the motivating factor. Psalms 118:24, "This is the day which the Lord hath made, we will rejoice and be glad in it."

Live by the Jesus's commandment to "love one another and Come Alive!

Dr. Mary Ann Echols recently shared one of several writings with me and she granted me permission to share this impactful insight with you.

COME ALIVE

I know that Jesus is alive and lives in me, but I sometimes live as if He is still in the tomb. When I lose faith, allow worry and fear to over-take me, lose control of my emotions, or think about giving up, I am forgetting that He rose again from the dead, is alive in me and has given me the power to overcome. (Isaiah 40:29).

I need Jesus, the risen Savior, to come alive in me and raise me up so I can be alive too. As I meet each day, I see how much of it slips away unnoticed. There are missed opportunities to serve the cause of Christ and missed connections that are linked to my spiritual assignment. It's as if I am going through the motions and not fully embracing the life God intended for me to live.

I need Jesus to come alive in me so that I can be aware of His presence in all things, large and

small and connect with the power inherent in His presence every minute, every hour, in every circumstance and in every relationship that hurts me. In His presence is the power I need to come alive and walk the path He has chosen for me.

I need Jesus to come alive in me so that my old wounds don't overtake the eternal joy and the peace He has given me (John 14:27). When He comes alive in me, I will have the strength to fight through pain and suffering. I will have enough love to forgive the unforgivable and I will have the faith to let the past stay in the past and dwell in the hope of the present (Romans 15:13). When Jesus comes alive in me I will recognize and celebrate the new thing He is doing in my life (Isaiah 43:19).

I need Jesus to come alive in me so that I can hear Him speak, discern the truth and apply God's wisdom to the challenges I will face today and every day (John 10:27). It is not enough for me to just read the Word of God it must come alive in me so that it spurs me into action. It will motivate me to do my part to change hearts and minds, starting with my own, so that the will of God will be fulfilled (James 1:25).

I need Jesus to come alive in me so that the distractions of life, i.e. work, bills, social media, etc. will not take the place of growing my relationship with Him. (Matthew 6:33). I need to experience more love and intimacy with God so I will truly know Him and see Him at work around me. I need Jesus to come live in me so that I become one with Him, the same power that led Him to obey the Father, carry His cross, suffer and die then be resurrected, will empower me to do the same (Matthew 16:24).

Instead of sinking into despair, I will pray for Him to come alive in me. I will embrace the healing restorative power that is available to me by His grace and mercy. Then, I know I will rise again with Christ to fight the good fight until He calls me home. (I Tim.6:12)"

The only thing that mattered was living a life that celebrates the love God has given me.

May God Bless You And Make You Whole.
Cheryl J. Bass-Foster

ABOUT THE AUTHOR

Luther and I celebrated our twenty-ninth wedding anniversary on November 16, 2020 and we are truly grateful for a blessed marriage. I am extremely grateful for the number of years that my husband has supported me in my journey. He has been a Trustee at our home church for over twenty six years and was blessed to be the church appointed photographer for several years. On November 3, 2019 he was ordained as a Deacon during an anointed sacred service.

I am excited about the dedication my husband has shown to love the Lord, love me as Christ loves the church, and my family and the church family. He is the real deal, there is nothing fake or phony about my husband. He functions in spite of his deafness in one ear.

I thank God for my supportive sister in love Erma Jean Hart, the heart and matriarch of the Foster family. Her kindness has always remained consistent.

Shawnie, my daughter, fulfilled a life-long prayer by graduating from Youngstown State University with a Bachelor's Degree in psychology. She has worked in the community for over twenty-five years and recently spear-headed several powerful spirit-filled events that turned into a spirit- filled experience within our community. She is the founder of T.H.R.I.V.E. and hosts Little Miss Inner Beauty Pageants, Mother-Daughter Community Teas and Warrior Woman Breakthrough to the New You 2018 Spiritual Warfare Conference. I received tremendous healings from assisting her and attending her God given ministries. God truly used her for His purposes in phenomenal ways and we're still asking God, "What Happened?"

My granddaughter, Maya, returned from Madrid and Barcelona, Spain, a life-long dream trip with her professor and eleven other students in their fashion design class for ten days. When we took her to the Pittsburgh Airport on May 12, 2019, it was so surreal how she's grown. She also traveled with her archaeology class to the Bahamas on December 14 – 23, 2019 where she explored caves. She was blessed to complete her studies at Youngstown State University during Covid19 coronavirus in May 2020. She has great compassion and has a great testimony on the miraculous healing power of God in her life. She contributed to my new perception and healing with the principle of Kintsugi.

My mother is still a blessing to me at 95 years old and enjoying her senior living in a beautiful assisted living facility. My siblings are healing and doing well. I celebrate the twenty –eighth anniversary of my sister, Denise's, victory and celebration of life.

And finally, I am joyful, peaceful and I am free even when I experience challenging circumstances. I have learned how to be quiet in God as he has taught me how to let go!

I marvel at the life that God has given back to me after experiencing great brokenness. I live every day, thankful for the small things. My quality of life is greatly improved and I still learn every day, I may have been broken, but now I am being made whole daily. There are times and areas that I will never have to experience brokenness again and have been Broken, But For the Last Time, and life happen which brings opportunities to grow in grace.

I can't thank God enough for the consistent impactful team ministry of Calvary Ministries International and Christ Church led by our Pastor, Sfg. Bishop C. Shawn Tyson and Evangelist Krista Tyson, that has kept us flowing in the Intentional Momentum of God during this season. In fact, Pastor Tyson wrote, Intentional Momentum, during this pandemic, and it's an excellent book.

I am thankful for their support and encouragement for a few of us who were able to receive a scholarship to become certified Mental Health Life Coaches with the American Association of Christian Counselors (AACC). God is yet in control and is preparing us for the new face of ministry in 2021.Amen.

CONTACT INFORMATION

Please feel free to contact Cheryl @ luthercheryl8@att.net.
Website - www.cherylbassfosterbooks